The Golden Lemon

The Golden Lemon

A Collection of Special Recipes

DORIS TOBIAS
and
MARY MERRIS

New York   Atheneum   1978

Recto stamping design by Richard Nagrowsky

Library of Congress Cataloging in Publication Data

Tobias, Doris.
   The golden lemon.
   Includes index.
   1. Cookery (Lemons)   I.   Merris, Mary, joint
author.   II.   Title.
   TX813.L4T6   641.6'4'334   77-88908
   ISBN 0-689-10860-5

TO ARTHUR AND BEL-GAZOU

for their loving support

CONTENTS

The Golden
Lemon

INTRODUCTION

We cannot imagine our kitchens without a basket of lemons on the windowsill.

In summer, they may share this basket with a mound of downy peaches. In winter, their companions are often a handful of papery shallots.

They remind us at all times of other places—a white-washed *auberge* in southern France, its terrace roofed in grape leaves— or a tiny inn jutting from the hills of Estoril above a glittering Atlantic, where lunch one blazing August noon was mussel stew, fragrant with lemon and garlic.

But our baskets of lemons do more than snatch a fragmented remembrance. They are often the mainstay of a memorable recipe and can elevate an ordinary dish into something sublime.

They sometimes add their pungency anonymously, are sometimes directly and purely lemon, and on occasion, as when they melt with garlic, form a third flavor.

Lemons, having an affinity with all types of dishes, give another dimension to good food. And the sharing of good food is, after all, one of the abiding joys of life.

We have included menu and wine suggestions with each recipe, but they are not intended to be rigid. We have simply indicated what we have found goes particularly well with these dishes. There is no rule that says you have to have a first course, entrée, vegetable, and dessert. If you prefer to serve a main course with just a splendid dessert, it can make a marvelous meal.

In most cases, we have suggested several wines, usually from different countries, that will go well with our special menus. But by all means, be guided by your own taste.

SOME NOTES ON LEMONS

The best lemons for juice and pulp are the small, round or oval ones, with smooth, unblemished skins. The smaller lemons tend to have fewer seeds, but this is really a matter of chance. Should seeds show up, they must always be removed.

Store lemons at room temperature in an airy basket if you are going to use them within a few days, because you obtain more juice from a lemon that is not cold. However, if you intend to keep the lemons for some time, they must be refrigerated. Immerse refrigerated lemons in hot water for a few minutes before using to extract the maximum amount of juice.

When a recipe calls for lemon peel, or zest, which is the same thing, the best way to get the peel off without the bitter, white pith that lies between the skin and the pulp is to use a potato peeler. When grating, be careful also not to include the pith.

In our recipes, fresh lemon juice is always used.

GREAT WAYS WITH LEMON

• Squeeze fresh lemon juice over sautéed zucchini just before serving.

• Sprinkle sautéed carrot rounds with grated lemon rind and grated onion.

• Drizzle fresh lemon juice over eggs that have been scrambled with a bit of garlic; smother with chopped Italian parsley.

• Keep a mandoline slicer for wafer-thin lemon slices.

• Stud a whole lemon with cloves and tie with a blue velvet ribbon for a pomander ball.

• Keep a crock of lemon butter in the refrigerator, ready to sauce fresh vegetables, fish, or poached chicken breasts.

• Mix grated lemon peel with finely minced parsley and garlic and sprinkle over veal shanks, sautéed veal scallops, or broiled filet mignon.

• Rub the cut side of a lemon half over eggshell surfaces before boiling to avoid cracking.

• Add 1 tablespoon finely grated lemon peel, 2 teaspoons fresh lemon juice, and 2 tablespoons confectioners' sugar to a pint of whipped sweet cream. Serve over warm crêpes.

• Rub a bunch of fresh parsley or mint leaves with some lemon peel between your palms after slicing garlic or onions.

• Drop a lemon wedge into simmering, homemade tomato sauce for pasta.

• Throw in a cut lemon half when cooking cauliflower to keep it white and eliminate odors.

• Make your own lemon jelly. Put in French hinged jars and wrap with blue tissue paper and yellow ribbons for gifts.

• Make your own lemon chutney. Spoon into small glass jars with cork closures. Make pretty name labels for the jars.

• Keep a jar of lemon butterscotch sauce in the refrigerator for fruits and ice cream.

• Pile lemons in a shallow, handwoven basket and spike with white daisies for a centerpiece.

• Tie lemon halves in a cheesecloth bag when serving fish or other dishes to avoid pits.

- Serve a lemon wedge with vichyssoise. It does things for it.
- Add curls of lemon peel to your favorite potpourri.
- Place thick strips of lemon peel in a warm oven for a few minutes to dispel unwanted odors.
- Freeze lemonade ice cubes. Add to tall fruit juice drinks or Campari and soda.
- Do buy a good lemon juicer, such as a French wood cone or corrugated cone in a bowl. In an emergency, squeeze a lemon half around the tines of a fork.

FIRST COURSES

LEMON SOUP

We like our lemon soup to be nicely enriched with eggs, with a strong sense of lemon. We add a few tablespoons of rice while the soup is being prepared, but it all passes through a sieve at the end, so the rice becomes a creamy thickening agent.

The lemon soup makes a lovely luncheon entrée, either hot or cold, accompanied with garlic or Parmesan bread. As a first course, follow it with broiled pork chops in Madeira sauce and fresh green beans. For dessert, a frozen chestnut pudding garnished with whole glacéed chestnuts.

WINE SUGGESTION: A dry, sparkling white wine, such as a non-vintage French champagne or an American sparkling wine.

> 6 cups defatted chicken stock
> 4 eggs and 2 egg yolks
> ½ cup lemon juice
> ¼ teaspoon salt
> 2 tablespoons long grain rice

Warm the stock in a saucepan. Beat eggs and egg yolks until light and mix in the lemon juice and salt. Pour a small amount of the warm chicken stock into the egg mixture, whisking rapidly while it is being added. Continue adding spoonfuls of the stock to the egg mixture, stirring all the while, until the egg mixture is warm. It can then be poured back into the remaining stock without danger of curdling. Whisk mixture well, add the 2 tablespoons of rice, and simmer, stirring occasionally, for 20 minutes. Strain the soup through a sieve, pressing enough of the soft rice through to thicken it slightly. Whisk again so that the soup is smooth and creamy.

SERVES FOUR.

POTAGE AUBERGINE
(Eggplant Soup)

The plump purple eggplants that are the base for this soup are baked, puréed, and cooked with fresh tomatoes, beef stock enriched with lemon, and a little Cognac. This unusual soup makes a fine fall luncheon entrée, with plenty of fresh crusty rye bread and country sweet butter. Serve the soup in large Italianate bowls and pass plenty of freshly grated Romano cheese. It doubles as the first course at dinner, served in small, delicate porcelain cups. Follow with duckling cut into serving pieces, treated with a hail of cracked black pepper and broiled until crisp. With the duckling, serve a salad of bibb lettuce in a winey vinaigrette dressing. For dessert, a pear pie.

WINE SUGGESTION: A fruity but mature Beaujolais, such as Brouilly or Morgon.

One 3-pound or two 1½-pound eggplants (to make 2 cups purée)
8 or 9 fresh, ripe tomatoes (to make 1 cup purée)
3 basil leaves

1 quart rich beef stock or broth
1 medium-sized onion, grated
3 tablespoons lemon juice
Salt and freshly ground pepper to taste

2 sprigs fresh thyme or ⅛
   teaspoon dried
1 teaspoon fresh tarragon,
   chopped, or
¼ teaspoon dried

⅛ teaspoon ground
   allspice
¼ cup Cognac
Grated Romano cheese

Preheat oven to 450° F.

Prick the skins of the eggplants in a few places and place on a cookie sheet or pan. Bake 1 hour or longer, until the flesh is soft when tested with the tines of a long fork. Remove from oven, cool, peel, and chop pulp; or put it through a food mill. If you don't like seeds, push the pulp through a fine sieve. Measure 2 cups of purée and reserve.

Skin the tomatoes and cut them in half. Squeeze each half gently to remove seeds, and chop coarsely. Place the tomatoes and basil leaves in a heavy saucepan and cook over medium heat, stirring, until the liquid has been reduced and the pulp is rich and saucy. Measure 1 cup of the purée and turn it into a 2½- or 3-quart kettle. Add the puréed eggplant and stir to blend. Place the eggplant-tomato purée over medium heat. Add the beef stock, grated onion, lemon juice, salt and pepper, thyme, tarragon, and allspice and cook, stirring from time to time, for 40 minutes. Add Cognac and cook for another 5 minutes.

SERVES THREE AS A LUNCHEON ENTRÉE, OR SIX AS A FIRST COURSE.

CARROT SOUP

Lemon juice transforms a simple carrot soup into a lovely beginning to a meal. It could be followed by *noisettes* (little rounds of lamb) cut from the loin that are grilled until crisp outside and still pink within. Mushroom caps sautéed in a little lemon and butter make a nice garniture. Accompany this with Idaho potatoes cut in half, coated with melted butter and a little sweet paprika, turned cut side down onto a cookie sheet and baked until crusty, about 35 minutes in a hot oven. For dessert, a salad of fresh seasonal fruits—tangerine segments, fresh pineapple cubes, and slivers of unpeeled apples and pears laced with kirsch.

WINE SUGGESTION: An elegant and assertive medium-bodied red, such as a Santaney or Mercurey from Burgundy, or a red Graves.

3 cups carrots, peeled and thinly
    sliced
3 cups water
3 tablespoons lemon juice
Salt and white pepper to taste

4 heaping teaspoons dairy
    sour cream
1 tablespoon fresh dillweed
    or 1 teaspoon dried

Slice carrots rather thin so they'll cook more quickly. Place them in a 2½-quart saucepan, cover with water, bring to a boil, and boil briskly from 10 to 12 minutes, until carrots are tender but not mushy. Skim off the orange foam that forms on the top. Remove from heat and cool slightly. Turn the carrots and the water into a blender or the bowl of a food processor, add the lemon juice, salt and white pepper, and process until puréed and light. You can see the carrots brightening in color as they whirr. Return soup to stove and reheat just until it reaches a boil. Ladle into prewarmed small bowls or soup cups—white is a pretty foil for the orange. Garnish each with the sour cream and chopped dill.

    To serve cold, chill the soup after you have completed the puréeing.

SERVES FOUR.

Note: This soup really requires a good blender or food processor. If you don't own one, you will need to push the cooked carrots and water through a sieve, add the lemon juice, salt and pepper, and proceed as above.

CHINESE MELON SOUP

Offbeat and refreshing, this soup makes an appropriate start to a Chinese meal—or a perfect beginning to any meal. It may be prepared ahead and reheated, but it's so easy to put together you can have it ready in minutes. Follow the melon soup with a stir-fry of chicken breasts cut into thin strips and quickly sautéed in a little oil with Chinese pea pods, water chestnuts, and dried mushrooms, accented with light soy sauce and a dash of sherry. Serve plain boiled rice. For dessert, Chinese kumquats and freshly brewed oolong tea.

WINE SUGGESTION: A dry, light white California Fumé Blanc.

6 cups rich chicken stock	3 dried Chinese black
3 cups sweet, ripe cantaloupe,	mushrooms, soaked in
peeled, seeded, and cubed	water for 10 minutes,
or diced	drained and diced
½ cup lemon juice	Freshly ground pepper
1 tablespoon light soy sauce	to taste

Place chicken stock, cantaloupe, lemon juice, and soy sauce in a saucepan. Bring to a boil, then lower flame. Add diced mushrooms and a few grindings of pepper, and simmer for 10 minutes.

Pour into pretty porcelain soup bowls and serve at once.
SERVES FOUR.

POTAGE FROID AUX POIREAUX
(Chilled Cream of Leek Soup)

Chilled cream of leek soup is a delicious way to start off lunch or dinner on a warm day. It's vaguely reminiscent of that soup with the French name, vichyssoise—which was created in America by Louis Diat—but calls for no potatoes or heavy cream.

Serve the soup well chilled, in small porcelain soup cups. It sets the mood for a light and lovely luncheon entrée of salade Niçoise, that wonderful mélange of greens, tuna, black olives, anchovies, tomatoes, and herbs of Provence tossed with a light French olive oil and lemon juice. Have a basket of crusty French bread and a pot of country sweet butter on the table. For dessert, fresh ripe peaches and a triple crème cheese, such as Saint Hubert.

WINE SUGGESTION: A well-chilled rosé from Provence or a California Rosé of Cabernet makes enchanting summer sipping.

3 fresh leeks about 1 inch in diameter	1 cup sour cream
3 cups chicken stock	¼ cup lemon juice
3 cups buttermilk	Salt and freshly ground pepper to taste

Trim the root ends of the leeks and slice off most of the green parts. Slit the remaining green part of the leeks crosswise for a few inches. Wash them thoroughly under running water to get

out every bit of sand or earth that clings. Drain the leeks, place
them in a small saucepan, and cover them with chicken stock. If
they're not completely covered, add additional stock or water to
cover. Bring to a boil, lower heat, and simmer until tender, for
about 10 to 15 minutes, then drain. (Save the cooking liquid to
cook other vegetables.) Place the leeks in the container of a
blender or food processor, and purée. Add the remaining ingredients, process until the mixture is well blended and smooth, then
taste to correct seasoning. Chill well before serving. The soup may
be garnished with finely minced chives or parsley.

SERVES FOUR.

COLD MELON SOUP

On a hot summer day, a bowl of this light, cold soup is wonderfully refreshing. Unlike the hot Chinese melon soup, the cantaloupe in this version is puréed with lots of lemon, a good
amount of Cognac, and spiked with tiny bits of fresh ginger.

Serve the soup as a first course for supper or as a luncheon
entrée with hot *gougère,* a crusty cheese bread.

Try the same formula using honeydew, casaba, or Persian
melon for tasteful variations.

4 cups chilled, ripe cantaloupe, peeled, seeded, and cubed
⅔ cup lemon juice, chilled
Salt and freshly ground pepper to taste
⅓ cup Cognac
½ teaspoon fresh ginger, finely minced (or ¼ teaspoon
powdered)

Place all ingredients in the container of a blender or food processor and process until liquid and foamy. Pour into glass mugs or bowls and serve at once. If desired, an ice cube or two may be tucked into each bowl.

SERVES TWO FOR LUNCH; FOUR AS A FIRST COURSE.

AVOCADO BISQUE

Little chunks of fresh green avocado give special taste and texture to this easily assembled bisque. It is elegant when served hot, garnished with a few crisp croutons, and it's delightful when served chilled. Either way, the soup is a lovely meal starter. Follow with whole, boned striped bass baked with a stuffing of finely minced, fresh mushrooms, thinly sliced onions, and wafer-thin slices of fresh zucchini, basted with dry white wine and lemon juice. Serve fluffy boiled rice with the fish to catch the delicious pan juices. A nice vegetable garnish with the fish would be whole cherry tomatoes baked in a *cocotte* with butter and finely minced basil. For dessert, a coconut layer cake.

WINE SUGGESTION: A well-chilled, light, fruity white varietal, such as a California Chenin Blanc or a flowery soft German Moselle.

½ cup lemon juice
1 large avocado
Salt and freshly ground pepper to taste
1½ cups rich chicken broth
¾ cup heavy cream

Pour the lemon juice into a deep bowl. Peel and pit the avocado, cut it into large chunks, and dip them immediately into the lemon juice. With a fork, mash the avocado in the lemon juice—not too finely, as you want some of the pulp to remain in nuggets about the size of a pea. Season with salt and pepper. Turn the mixture into a saucepan, preferably one with an enamel lining, and place over low heat. Slowly add the chicken broth, stirring to blend, then add the heavy cream. Bring the soup just to a boil and simmer for 2 minutes. Serve hot or chill in the refrigerator for several hours.

SERVES TWO.

FRESH BEET SOUP

The brilliant claret red of the beets is tempered with pure white sour cream, which transmutes it to a heavenly pink. Snippets of feathery green dill and matchsticks of raw beet provide a lovely garnish. This is not the traditional borscht, since no eggs are used. The soup should be served well chilled, in delicate white china bowls, accompanied by dark pumpernickel bread and country sweet butter. Make it the focal point of a no-fuss luncheon on a broiling summer day, with a platter of cheeses and a basket of varied seasonal fruits. In cold weather, serve it hot. Pass the sour cream separately, at table.

At dinner, follow the soup with fresh tuna or swordfish slices broiled with butter, lemon, and a little oregano, broccoli flowers steamed, drained, and coated with a light vinaigrette, and little new potatoes, scrubbed, boiled in their jackets, tossed with a little lemon juice, salt, freshly ground pepper, and rolled in a liberal mound of freshly chopped Italian parsley. For dessert, thin crêpes rolled around sweet apricot purée and chopped hazlenuts.

WINE SUGGESTION: With the tuna or swordfish, a bone-dry white wine, such as a French or California Fumé Blanc.

2 bunches young beets, about 8 to 10 medium sized	Juice of 1 small lemon
½ small yellow onion, grated	1 teaspoon sugar
Salt and freshly ground pepper to taste	1 pint sour cream
1 quart chicken stock	1 raw beet, peeled and grated for garnish
	Freshly snipped dill

Peel beets, trim off ends, and cut into julienne sticks, either in a food processor or by hand. (The beets may be grated, but this gives the soup a different texture.) Turn the beets into a 2-quart saucepan; add grated onion, salt and pepper, and chicken stock. Bring to a boil, lower heat, cover, and simmer for 30 minutes, until beets are tender. Add lemon juice and sugar, taste to correct seasoning, and cool. Blend in the sour cream and chill the soup for several hours. When ready to serve, ladle into individual china bowls; add a little of the raw beet and a small cascade of freshly chopped dill to each serving.

SERVES FOUR AS A FIRST COURSE.

SORREL SOUP

European in origin and tangy-tart in flavor, sorrel soup makes a revitalizing hot-weather beverage. Serve it icy cold in mugs as an after-tennis, golf, or anytime refresher. Have a bowl as a luncheon entrée, with thickly sliced rye bread and sweet butter. Follow it with a platter of deviled eggs, tomato halves dusted with finely chopped basil leaves, freshly ground pepper and a bit of olive oil, and tiny black olives and crisp red radishes. For dessert, a pastry shell filled with crème Anglais under a layer of red raspberries.

WINE SUGGESTION: A chilled, dry white wine, such as a French Mâcon-Blanc Villages.

1 pound sorrel leaves, washed, stems off, and finely chopped	½ teaspoon salt
	A few grindings of fresh pepper
1 small bunch scallions (5 or 6), finely chopped	Juice of 1 lemon
	1 tablespoon sugar
1 quart chicken stock	2 eggs, well beaten

Place chopped sorrel leaves and scallions in a 2-quart saucepan. Add stock, bring to a boil, lower heat, and simmer for 45 minutes, stirring occasionally. Remove from heat, add seasonings, lemon juice, and sugar, and cool slightly. Beat eggs with a wire whisk until well blended, then stir them into the soup. Transfer soup to a covered container and chill for several hours. Serve in glass bowls or mugs. Pass a bowl of crème fraîche or sour cream separately.

SERVES FOUR.

COLD CUCUMBER SOUP

The best soups are those which capture the essence of the main ingredient. In this case, fresh cucumbers are peeled, seeded, and tossed into the blender with a little lemon juice and sour cream and a bit of minced shallot. The result is pure cucumber and very fresh.

Something this light could be followed by sautéed brains with butter and caper sauce, and broiled tomato slices. For dessert, brioche with a custard sauce. When we were first in France, we were served this family-style brioche. A large, slightly sweet brioche was passed around the table and each person pulled off the amount desired. Then a custard sauce was passed in a big bowl for each to douse his brioche accordingly. It's a pleasant custom and a lovely way to share dessert.

WINE SUGGESTION: A full-bodied Mâcon Blanc from France or a California Chardonnay.

3 good-sized cucumbers
3 tablespoons lemon juice
1 tablespoon shallots, minced
½ cup sour cream

Peel cucumbers with a potato peeler, slice them in half, and scoop out seeds with a spoon. Cut into chunks and toss them into a blender with the lemon juice and minced shallots. When puréed, add sour cream to the blender mixture and whirr until all is amalgamated.

SERVES TWO.

WHITE GAZPACHO

We were first introduced to this sensuously silken, unusual white gazpacho by Orlando Rodriguez in his Spanish restaurant, Alicante. Unlike the more familiar Andalusian gazpacho, with its strong red color and flavors, this variant from the region, Alicante, on the eastern coast of Spain and named the White Coast for its brilliant light, is paler in color and more subtle in flavor. It calls for not-too-ripe tomatoes, cucumber, and an olio of other fresh ingredients. Serve the well-chilled soup in deep bowls, with a tray of attractive garnishes, as a splendid summer luncheon entrée. It needs only crusty rolls, sweet butter, and wedges of Fontina cheese to make a satisfying summer midday meal. Or serve the white gazpacho in cups as an elegant first course at dinner. This could be followed by an entrée of striped bass grilled with fennel and steamed saffron rice. For dessert, a Spanish flan.

WINE SUGGESTION: A medium-dry, Spanish white wine, such as a white Rioja, would make excellent sipping.

1 large cucumber, peeled and coarsely chopped
3 medium-sized tomatoes, not too ripe, peeled, seeded, and chopped
2 tablespoons onions, coarsely chopped
2 small cloves garlic, chopped
4 slices white bread, crusts removed, cubed
2 extra large eggs
4 tablespoons olive oil
¼ cup lemon juice
2 cups cold water
Salt and freshly ground white pepper to taste

Place all ingredients in the container of a food processor or a blender and process until puréed and smooth. (If you use a blender, you may need to blend the ingredients in several installments.) Chill the soup at least 4 hours. Stir well before pouring into cups or bowls. Pass the garnishes in small bowls set on a pretty tray.

GARNISHES

Finely minced green pepper
Chopped hard-cooked eggs
Toasted homemade croutons
Thinly sliced scallions
Finely chopped red radishes

SERVES TWO AS A LUNCHEON ENTRÉE, FOUR IN SMALL CUPS AS A DINNER FIRST COURSE.

FONDS D'ARTICHAUTS GRATINES
(Stuffed Artichoke Bottoms)

Ground veal and pork are cooked with lemon juice, bound with a Mornay sauce, and piled into artichoke bottoms in this first-course dish. Actually, it's so good we often double the recipe and use it as an entrée.

As a first course it is somewhat rich, so what follows should be fairly simple, perhaps a delicate fish mousse with a thin, fresh tomato sauce and glazed carrots. For dessert, poached peaches with raspberry sauce.

WINE SUGGESTION: A light, elegant white wine, such as an Alsatian Riesling or a California Johannesburg Riesling.

THE ARTICHOKES

2 tablespoons butter	1 teaspoon salt
1 cup onions, chopped	8 artichoke bottoms,
½ pound ground veal	canned or fresh
½ pound ground pork	cooked
½ cup lemon juice	

THE MORNAY SAUCE

3 tablespoons butter	¾ cup Parmesan or
3 tablespoons flour	Gruyère cheese,
2 cups hot milk	grated

Preheat oven to 350° F.

Melt 2 tablespoons butter, add chopped onions, and cook until the onions are limp. Then add veal and pork, which have been mixed together, and stir-cook over medium heat for a few minutes until the meat loses color. Add lemon juice and salt and continue cooking the meat mixture, uncovered, over low heat for 30 minutes.

Meanwhile, make the Mornay sauce. Melt the 3 tablespoons of butter and add flour. Stir until smooth and let the mixture cook until it starts to bubble. Cook for 1 minute at this stage and remove from heat. The flour and butter must not brown, so regulate the heat to maintain a slight bubbling for the 1 minute. Let flour and butter mixture rest off the heat until bubbling subsides. Add milk, which has been brought just to the boiling point, stirring constantly while milk is being added. Return to heat and cook until mixture thickens.

Reserve 2 tablespoons of the grated cheese and add the remainder to the white sauce, stirring over low heat until cheese has melted.

Save ¾ cup of the Mornay sauce and stir what remains into the veal-pork mixture.

Arrange the artichoke bottoms in a buttered baking pan and fill them with the sauced meat. It doesn't matter if the filling flows over the edges—in fact, it's almost more delicious if the filling doesn't rest perfectly in the artichoke bases.

Pour reserved Mornay sauce over the 8 filled artichoke bottoms and sprinkle with the 2 tablespoons of grated cheese. Put in the preheated oven until warmed through and the top is slightly browned or place under broiler for a few minutes.

SERVES FOUR AS A FIRST COURSE.

STUFFED ARTICHOKES

Neatly trimmed artichokes, stuffed with prosciutto ham and parsley, and sauced with a lemon-onion-stock reduction, make a delicious first course.

They also make an attractive addition to an antipasto platter and are great for picnics because they pack well and can be eaten gracefully without benefit of knife and fork. Stuffed artichokes are a nice alternative to the traditional way of serving the artichoke whole, with either melted butter or mayonnaise, and this version can be varied. The initial preparation should be the same, but at the final stuffing, you could substitute barely-cooked garden peas and dill for the prosciutto and parsley. Sautéed, chopped mushrooms and minced, fried bacon or ham could be yet another choice.

On a picnic, the stuffed artichokes pair well with cold, stuffed, chicken breasts that have been sliced. (See page 75.) As a first course, follow with duckling roasted to crispness and served with plum sauce. Steamed zucchini matchsticks tossed with lemon and butter make a pleasant garniture. For dessert, a glazed orange tart.

WINE SUGGESTION: A young Beaujolais would be fine for both the duck and the picnic menu.

4 large artichokes	⅓ cup prosciutto ham,
2 tablespoons olive oil	finely chopped
4 tablespoons onion, minced	⅓ cup parsley, finely
1 garlic clove, minced	chopped
¼ cup lemon juice	1 tablespoon butter
1 cup chicken stock	

Prepare artichokes by cutting off the stems flush with the base and pulling off all tough exterior leaves. Then place the artichokes on their sides and cut off the top half of the leaves. You will be left with trimmed artichokes about 2 inches high. Cut each in half.

Warm olive oil in a pan that will accommodate the 8 artichoke halves. Add minced onion and garlic and cook briefly, about 2 minutes. Add lemon juice and chicken stock and bring to a boil. Add the artichoke halves, cover, and maintain at a low boil for approximately 40 minutes, or until a leaf slips off easily.

Remove artichokes and turn them upside down on paper towels to drain. When cool, remove chokes—the fuzzy centers—with a spoon. Boil the sauce until reduced and thickened, then add the prosciutto, parsley, and butter. Stir until blended. With a spoon, insert the mixture between the leaves of the artichokes and into the little hollows where the choke was removed. Serve hot or at room temperature.

SERVES FOUR.

GOLDEN LEMON FISH MOUSSE

It's hard to believe that this shimmeringly silken mousse, with its elegant appearance and wonderfully fresh flavor, is so uncomplicated to put together—but it is. The glossy white fillets of fish are perfumed with their own fresh juices and beaten with lemon juice—which enhances their freshness—egg whites for lightness, and an enrichment of heavy cream. Served hot and embellished with a thin, tangy tomato sauce (see page 28), the mousse makes an elegant first course. It could be followed by loin lamb chops grilled until crisp outside and pink and succulent within, served with a garniture of whole green beans sautéed in butter just until crunchy. For dessert, seasonal pears poached in white wine and a platter of almond crescent cookies.

The mousse also makes an exquisite cold luncheon entrée. Refrigerate until ready to serve, then slice as you would a pâté. Garnish the platter or plates with a few sprigs of leafy dark green watercress and cherry tomatoes. Serve crusty rolls and a pot of sweet butter.

WINE SUGGESTION: A light and elegant dry white wine, such as a California Johannesburg Riesling or a French Meursault with the mousse. With the lamb chops, a full-bodied red Bordeaux.

1½ pounds perfectly fresh
   fillets of flounder
1 small onion, finely grated
½ cup lemon juice
Whites of 2 extra large eggs

⅓ teaspoon salt
Freshly ground white
   pepper to taste
1 cup heavy cream

When selecting the fish, make sure you choose fillets that are glossy, shining, and absolutely white and fresh. This is essential to the quality of the mousse. Don't hesitate to smell the fillets. They should smell fresh and sweet.

Preheat oven to 350° F. Lightly butter a 2-quart soufflé dish.

If you own a food processor (see Note), cut the fish into chunks and process, using the sharp blade, until you have a smooth paste. Add grated onion, lemon juice, and process until well blended. Then add egg whites, salt and pepper, blending until smooth, and, finally, the heavy cream. The mixture should look white and appetizing. Use a spatula to scrape out every bit, and turn into the greased soufflé dish. Smooth the top with the spatula, cover snugly with aluminum foil or a lid that fits tightly, and set in a deep pan. Pour hot water into the pan to reach a half-inch below the top of the soufflé dish. Bake in the preheated oven for 50 to 60 minutes, until set. Carefully remove the soufflé dish from the water bath, set it on a heat-proof dish, and, using a large spoon, serve right from the dish. If you prefer to unmold the mousse, carefully place a heavy platter over the top of the baked soufflé, grasp the soufflé dish firmly—using potholders or heavy towels— and turn it upside down. Gently lift the soufflé dish. Garnish the top of the mousse with sprigs of feathery green dill and slice at table. Pass the tomato sauce.

SERVES SIX TO EIGHT.

Note: If you don't own a food processor, ask the fish dealer to grind the fish, using the finest blade. Turn the fish mixture into a large bowl. Add the lemon juice, grated onion, salt and pepper, egg whites, and beat well with an electric beater. Finally, add the heavy cream, continuing to beat until well blended and light. Proceed as above.

TOMATO SAUCE FOR GOLDEN LEMON MOUSSE

1¼ cups fresh tomatoes, peeled, seeded, and puréed in a blender or food processor

3 tablespoons lemon juice

1 tablespoon dill, finely chopped or ¼ teaspoon dried dillweed

Salt and freshly ground pepper to taste

1 tablespoon butter

Combine all ingredients except the butter and simmer in a small saucepan for 15 minutes. Then add the butter, swirl and stir until blended, and pour into a heated sauceboat.

SCALLOPS SASHIMI
(Raw Scallops in Lemon Juice)

The sweet essences of fresh bay scallops are heightened by a bath of lemon juice, olive oil, a fat clove of garlic, and a generous clump of minced parsley. The slices of absolutely fresh raw scallops are gently "cooked" by the lemon juice. The olive oil tempers the acidity of the lemon; the garlic and freshly snipped parsley add flavor.

Serve scallops sashimi as a first course with thin, crisp bread, followed by a roast of veal and sautéed carrots. For dessert, whole fresh strawberries and crème fraîche.

WINE SUGGESTION: A bone-dry but assertive white wine, such as Pouilly Fumé or Muscadet from the Loire Valley, served well chilled.

1 pound bay scallops	½ cup olive oil
1 teaspoon salt	1 large clove garlic, split
Freshly ground black pepper to	in half
taste	½ cup curly parsley, finely
½ cup lemon juice	chopped

Rinse scallops, pat dry, and slice into thin rounds. Place in a shallow ceramic or glass dish. Season with salt and freshly ground pepper, pour lemon juice and olive oil over them, and add garlic halves. Stir gently with a spoon. Marinate at room temperature for at least 1½ hours. Serve at once, or if you wish to prepare these ahead of time, cover and place them in the refrigerator until ready to serve.

SERVES FOUR.

STEAK TARTARE WITH LEMON

There are countless versions of steak tartare, but we think this one, a recipe from Charles Mount, American artist, architect and cook, is simply super. It may be served for many occasions—as a first course, as a luncheon or brunch main course, or as a sumptuous addition to an antipasto platter for the buffet table.

As a luncheon or brunch entrée, serve the steak tartare with a salad of sliced, red-ripe tomatoes, drizzled with a light French olive oil, and flecked with freshly snipped basil leaves. Add a warmed, crusty French or Italian loaf with a pot of country sweet butter. For dessert, along with the bread and butter, a bowl of beautiful seasonal pears and a choice of cheeses, such as Saint André, Italian Fontina, and a salty Bryndza from Roumania.

As a buffet table centerpiece, arrange the steak tartare in a round or oblong shape on a pretty platter. Score the top of the meat in a diamond pattern, using a sharp knife, and dust the top with finely chopped parsley combined with grated lemon zest. Garnish the platter with lemon quarters, clusters of shiny black Italian olives, and red radishes. Add a basket of thinly sliced rye and pumpernickel breads.

As a first course or as an addition to an antipasto platter, mound the meat on leaves of Boston lettuce. Add slices of Genoa salami, pink prosciutto ham, and slices of casaba melon, fresh mushroom caps marinated in a light vinaigrette, artichoke bottoms filled with tiny new peas, cooked shrimp in a mustardy mayonnaise, icy-crisp red radishes, sticks of raw carrot poked into pitted Spanish olives, and tiny black Italian olives.

WINE SUGGESTION: Châteauneuf-du-Pape, a robust red wine from the hot and sunny climate of the Rhone Valley in France, whose full flavor makes it eminently suitable to the steak tartare.

½ cup capers, coarsely chopped	½ cup green onion tops,
1 cup white Bermuda onion,	coarsely chopped
finely chopped	

½ cup fresh Italian parsley,
coarsely chopped
2 large cloves garlic, finely
minced or pressed
4 tablespoons Dijon mustard
2 tablespoons horseradish,
grated
3 tablespoons
Worcestershire sauce
½ teaspoon hot pepper
sauce
6 anchovy fillets, finely
chopped

3 pounds chopped or
coarsely ground sirloin
steak or tenderloin,
with all the fat re-
moved. If you can
handchop the steak or
use a food processor,
so much the better
3 raw eggs
½ cup lemon juice
Rind of ½ lemon, finely
grated
Freshly ground pepper
and salt to taste

In a large mixing bowl, mix the capers, onion and green tops, parsley, garlic, mustard, and horseradish. Add to the mixture the Worcestershire sauce, hot pepper sauce, and the anchovy fillets. Combine and transfer to a small bowl. Clean the mixing bowl you've just used. Place the ground or chopped steak in the mixing bowl. Add the eggs and mix well; add the lemon juice and the rind and mix well; add the capers-onion-horseradish mixture to the steak mixture and mix well. Season with freshly ground pepper and salt to taste.

SERVES THIRTY AT BUFFET.

VARIATION

Here's the recipe for four for lunch or brunch.

2 tablespoons capers, coarsely chopped

⅓ cup onion, finely chopped

2 tablespoons green onion tops, coarsely chopped

3 tablespoons fresh parsley, coarsely chopped

½ clove garlic, finely chopped or pressed

1 tablespoon Dijon mustard

2 teaspoons horseradish, grated

1 tablespoon Worcester-shire sauce

A few dashes hot-pepper sauce

2 anchovy fillets, finely chopped

1¼ pounds chopped or coarsely ground sirloin steak or tenderloin

1 raw egg

¼ cup lemon juice

½ teaspoon lemon rind, grated

Freshly ground pepper and salt to taste

Proceed as for larger amount.

EMINCE CRU FILET DE BOEUF AUX HERBES
(Marinated Raw Beef with Herbs)

This is one of the appetizers included in the expensive prix-fixe dinner served at The Palace restaurant in New York. It will cost you appreciably less to prepare this at home, and it needn't be limited to a first course. The thin slices of beef marinated in a mustard and caper oil dressing also make a nice addition to a buffet table. Or serve it as a light Sunday night supper entrée with a large salad of seasonal greens, tomato wedges, tiny black olives, and diced hardcooked eggs. Add a basket of warm, crusty Italian bread and fresh sweet butter. For dessert, a rich, moist chocolate cake and plenty of steaming espresso.

WINE SUGGESTION: A sturdy, robust red, such as Italian Barolo or a Côtes du Rhone.

2 cups pure green Sicilian
    olive oil
⅔ cup French wine vinegar
Salt and freshly ground pepper
    to taste
¼ cup capers, drained and
    chopped
½ teaspoon Dijon mustard

3 tablespoons chopped
    fresh fines herbes—
    parsley, chives, shallots,
    chervil, tarragon
Juice of 1 large lemon
1 pound prime filet
    mignon, thinly sliced
    and pressed flat to
    ⅛-inch thick
Lemon wedges for garnish

In a glass bowl combine olive oil, vinegar, salt, pepper, capers, mustard, and herbs and beat with a wire whisk until well blended. Add the lemon juice and beat until blended. Taste, and season with more salt and pepper if needed.

Place the thin slices of filet mignon in a shallow pan large enough to hold them without overlapping. Pour the marinade over the slices and permit the meat to marinate at room temperature for a half-hour. When ready to serve, place 4 slices of meat on each chilled plate. Garnish with lemon wedges. Pass the pepper mill.

SERVES FOUR.

CRUDITES WITH DIPPING SAUCE
(Raw Vegetables with Sauce)

Crudités is the French word for raw vegetables or fruits. But this splendid dish is too fresh and appetizing to be called by pedestrian-sounding English equivalent. Only young, tender, perfect specimens are entitled to be part of this attractive grouping, so you really must hand-pick the vegetables. It's especially important to select pencil-thin, young asparagus for their sweet, crunchy flavor and texture. If you can't find thin ones, substitute rutabaga cut into julienne strips. Serve the crudités on a large oval platter, surrounding the dip, as a first course at dinner. They also double as a light luncheon, accompanied by a robust cheese such as Taleggio or Bel Paese, crusty bread, and sweet butter.

WINE SUGGESTION: A not-too-dry, fruity white wine, such as a German Moselle or Swiss Fendent, served well chilled.

THE VEGETABLES

1 pound tiny, fresh white mushrooms
1 cup lemon juice
1 head fresh white cauliflower
2 heads fresh Belgian endive
3 fresh young carrots
1 pound tender young green beans

1 pound pencil-thin, fresh young asparagus
2 bunches crisp red radishes
1 large perfect green pepper

Select mushrooms that are absolutely fresh and white. Wipe mushrooms with a damp towel but don't peel them. Trim a tiny slice from the stems but leave stems on. Place ½ cup of the lemon juice in a bowl large enough to hold the mushrooms and add them as you wipe them off. Shake the bowl to make certain all the mushrooms are coated with lemon juice. Cover the bowl with plastic wrap and refrigerate until serving time.

Wash cauliflower and cut into individual flowerets. Add the flowerets to the remaining ½ cup of lemon juice in another bowl and shake the bowl to coat them well so that they will remain white. Cover with plastic wrap and refrigerate.

Wash Belgian endive and separate into leaves. Wrap in paper towels and refrigerate until ready to serve.

Scrape carrots and cut them into pencil-thin strips.

Wash green beans, trim off ends, place in a plastic bag, and refrigerate until ready to serve.

Cut off the woody ends of the asparagus and, using a vegetable peeler, carefully peel each stalk starting just below the bud tip. Place in a bowl, cover with cold water, and refrigerate until ready to serve.

Trim radishes but leave ¼-inch of green stem. With a small, sharp knife make petals, starting midway and slicing down to but not through the base. Place radish roses in a bowl of cold water and refrigerate until ready to serve.

Wash and dry the green pepper. Using a small, sharp paring knife cut the top of the pepper in a zigzag pattern about ½-inch from the top. Cut all around, as you would a pumpkin top. When the top is free, scrape away any seeds that may cling to it and set aside. Scoop out the inside of the pepper, getting rid of the sponge and its attached seeds, but be careful not to pierce the bottom which will serve as a container for the dipping sauce.

Wrap the pepper and its top in plastic and refrigerate until ready to serve.

THE DIPPING SAUCE

> 1 cup homemade lemon mayonnaise (see page 192)
> 1 tablespoon capers, well drained
> ½ teaspoon onion, finely grated
> 3 tablespoons red wine vinegar
> 3 tablespoons tomato purée

Combine all sauce ingredients in a small bowl and beat with a wooden spoon until blended. Taste for seasoning. You may like a bit more onion or an additional teaspoon of tomato purée. The sauce should be a lovely pink color. Cover well and refrigerate until ready to serve.

ASSEMBLAGE:

Have ready a large, round ceramic or glass platter. Or line a shallow, rectangular hand-woven basket with a napkin. Take all the vegetables from the refrigerator. Using paper towels, gently pat dry everything except the mushrooms and cauliflower. Remove the mushrooms and cauliflower from the lemon bath and drain, but don't pat them dry. Leave them with the lemon coating that remains after draining.

Spoon the dipping sauce into the scooped-out pepper and replace its lid. Set the pepper in the center of the platter or lined basket.

Pile the vegetables in groups, alternating deep and light colors, around the pepper.

SERVES TEN.

Note: Other vegetables you may add to the crudités tray, according to seasonal availability, are: cherry tomatoes; rutabaga, peeled and cut into thin slices; celery or fennel, cut lengthwise into spears; young, ice-water-crisped spinach leaves; curly chicory; sliced cucumbers and raw zucchini cut into thin sticks.

TAPANADE
(Tuna-Anchovy Sauce)

Capers, Italian olives, tuna, lemon juice, and Cognac are among the ingredients whisked together to make this sauce.

It can be served in a bowl with a stack of raw, young asparagus nearby for dipping. Or it can be used as a garnish for broiled fish, pork, or cold, boiled beef.

It's especially nice as a standby first course because the ingredients can be kept on hand in the cupboard. All you need are some raw or cold, cooked vegetables for dipping. Follow it with soft, scrambled eggs and sautéed chicken livers. For dessert, fresh figs flambéed with Curaçao and served with a pitcher of heavy cream.

WINE SUGGESTION: A light and charming red wine, such as a California Gamay Beaujolais, served slightly chilled.

¼ cup capers, drained	15 Italian black olives, pitted
One 2-ounce can anchovies, drained	Juice of 2 lemons
	¼ cup olive oil
One 7-ounce can tuna, drained	1 tablespoon Cognac

Place all ingredients except the olive oil and Cognac in a blender and blend until puréed. Keeping the blender on, add the olive oil in droplets until mixture is thick and creamy. Pour into serving dish and stir in the Cognac.

MAKES ABOUT 1½ CUPS.

FIVE EASY RAPÉS
(Grated Vegetable Appetizers)

Rapé is the French word for grated. These freshly grated vegetables tossed with lemon, oil, and herbs may be served as a light and crunchy first course, or on a luncheon plate accompanying sliced country ham, stuffed hard-cooked eggs, and crisp, warmed rolls and butter. They're also great to take on picnics and can be conveniently packed in lidded jars. To determine the type of shred you like best, try several grating sizes as a test. If you own a food processor, the shredding takes only seconds.

CARROT RAPÉ

2 cups carrots, grated
1 teaspoon onion, grated
Salt and freshly ground pepper to taste
½ cup light salad oil
¼ cup lemon juice

Scrape carrots and grate by hand or use the grating disc of a food processor. Turn shredded carrots into a large bowl and add grated onion, salt, pepper, salad oil, and lemon juice; toss lightly to blend

and chill. Serve mounded in a bowl or in individual lettuce cups.
SERVES EIGHT.

VARIATION

Add the following to the basic carrot rapé recipe:

> 1 cup green pepper, shredded
> 1 cup golden raisins
> 1 tablespoon fresh dill, finely minced

Toss with the carrot-onion rapé, add more salt and pepper if needed and chill.

BEET RAPÉ

2 cups beets (about 6 large large fresh beets), shredded	Salt and freshly ground pepper to taste
1 tablespoon onion, grated	¼ cup light salad oil
	¼ cup fresh lemon juice
	¼ cup fresh orange juice

Trim ends off and peel beets with a vegetable peeler. Shred or grate to desired size, place in a bowl, and toss with remaining ingredients. Chill well.
SERVES SIX.

RED AND WHITE CABBAGE RAPÉ

2 cups white cabbage, shredded
2 cups red cabbage, shredded
1 tablespoon onion, finely
grated
2 tablespoons caraway seeds

Salt and freshly ground
pepper to taste
½ cup lemon mayonnaise,
preferably homemade
(see page 192)
2 tablespoons lemon juice

Combine shredded cabbages, onion, caraway seeds, salt, and pepper. Blend mayonnaise with lemon juice. Add to the cabbage and toss lightly to blend. Chill.

SERVES EIGHT TO TEN.

CELERY-ROOT RAPÉ

1 large, fresh celery root
¼ cup lemon juice
1 to 2 tablespoons mild Dijon
mustard

½ cup homemade lemon
mayonnaise (see page
192)
Salt and freshly ground
pepper to taste

Select a large, firm celery root. Peel with a vegetable peeler and rub at once with a cut lemon half to prevent darkening. Grate by hand or in a food processor. Place immediately into a bowl and toss with the lemon juice. Combine mustard and mayonnaise, add to the celery root, and toss to blend thoroughly. Chill.

SERVES FOUR.

RADISH RAPÉ

1 pound black winter or white icicle radishes
1 teaspoon onion, finely grated
¼ cup lemon juice
¼ cup light salad oil
Salt and freshly ground pepper to taste

Those large, round, black-skinned radishes are best for this rapé, since they're pungent and bitey. Long white icicles are satisfactory, but their texture is more watery and the taste not as pungent. The red radishes look pretty when they're grated, with the red and white shreds intermingled . . . but again, they lose out in flavor and texture. In any case, serving radish rapé is unusual in itself, so if you can't find black or icicle radishes, try it with whatever radish is available.

Grate the radishes and toss them with the remaining ingredients. Chill well and serve with chicken liver pâté.

SERVES SIX.

MUSHROOMS IN LEMON-CREAM SAUCE

In this recipe mushrooms are cooked in a lemon-cream mixture until they have absorbed most of it. In the process, they exude their own juices and the result is a naturally thickened sauce that, when done, coats the mushrooms and tastes of the very essence of the three ingredients.

This can be served as a vegetable dish with roasts or chops, but is a nice first course served on small pastry rounds that have been dusted with Parmesan cheese and baked. If used as a first course, follow with grilled brook trout, scalloped potatoes, and baked tomatoes stuffed with spinach and cheese. For dessert, individual babas au rhum.

WINE SUGGESTION: A slightly chilled, fruity red wine, such as Beaujolais, with the mushrooms. A crisp white wine with some elegance, such as an Alsatian or German Riesling, with the trout.

> 1¼ pounds mushrooms
> Juice of 1 lemon
> 1 tablespoon butter
> 1 cup heavy cream
> ½ teaspoon salt

Wipe mushrooms, slice caps, and cut stems in half. If mushrooms are small, use them whole, but it is preferable to have at least medium-sized mushrooms that can be cut in half.

Sprinkle half the lemon juice onto the sliced mushrooms. Melt butter in a saucepan or large skillet and add mushrooms. Toss briefly until butter has been absorbed and mushrooms are slightly warm. Do not brown.

Pour cream over mushrooms, add salt and the remaining lemon juice. You can squeeze the juice right into the mixture but, of course, hold a strainer under the lemon if you do. Bring to a light boil and maintain, stirring occasionally, until mushrooms have absorbed most of the liquid, about 30 minutes. The sauce will have become quite thick and mocha colored. Spoon onto 8 pastry rounds.

SERVES FOUR.

CHAMPIGNONS PIQUANTS
(Pickled Mushrooms)

Drain these from their spicy marinade, pile them into a pretty bowl, and serve along with other crudités—raw vegetables—such as pencil slim, peeled asparagus stalks, cauliflowerets, cherry tomatoes, and carrot curls. Or place drained mushrooms in crisp green bibb lettuce leaves and serve as a light first course. Follow with leg of lamb roasted, Swedish style—basted with a cup of lightened and sweetened coffee—cooked lentils, and sautéed salsify. For dessert, oeufs à la neige—little puffs of meringue in a light custard sauce.

WINE SUGGESTION: A fairly mature, medium-bodied, red Bordeaux or a Cabernet Sauvignon from California.

1 pound small, fresh white mushrooms	½ teaspoon dried dillweed, or 2 to 3 sprigs fresh dill
1 cup lemon juice	
1 cup salad or olive oil	Salt and freshly ground pepper to taste
1 teaspoon pickling spice	
½ teaspoon chervil	2 cups water
½ teaspoon oregano	

Wipe mushrooms with damp paper towels. Leave stems on unless they are woody or brown, in which case, trim them. Place mushrooms in a saucepan. Add lemon juice, oil, spices, herbs, salt, pepper, and water. Bring to a boil, then turn off heat and cool. Pour mushrooms and marinade into a bowl; cover and refrigerate until ready to use. These may be prepared ahead, as they will keep up to a week when stored in their marinade.

SERVES FOUR AS AN APPETIZER, OR SIX ON A TRAY OF CRUDITÉS.

STUFFED MUSHROOMS

Unlike most stuffed mushroom recipes, this one does not use bread crumbs, garlic, or a mixture of cheeses. Grated lemon rind, parsley, Parmesan cheese and the chopped stems, bound with butter, are the only ingredients, and the result makes a fresh, light appetizer. They are excellent served with drinks and are nice accompanying a parsley-flecked omelet at lunch.

> 1 pound medium-sized mushrooms
> Grated rind of 3 lemons
> 5 tablespoons butter, melted
> 3 tablespoons parsley, minced
> 4 tablespoons Parmesan cheese, grated

Preheat oven to 350° F.

Try to select mushrooms that are uniform in size. Wipe them and remove stems. Mince the stems and combine with grated lemon rind. Sauté briefly in the melted butter until most of the butter has been absorbed. Add parsley and cheese and mix well. Using a teaspoon, stuff the caps and place in a well-buttered baking dish. Place in preheated oven for 15 minutes or until mushrooms have turned color and are warmed through.

SERVES SIX GENEROUSLY WITH COCKTAILS.

RICE SALAD I

The slightly medicinal flavor of saffron works well in this dish, which starts out as a risotto and ends up as a salad with chunks of poached chicken breasts and parsley. Serve it mounded on tender leaves of bibb lettuce as a first course, followed by grilled calves liver steaks and braised endive. For dessert, vanilla ice cream and blueberry sauce with a few candied violets on top would be appropriate.

The rice salad would also be a pleasant main course for luncheon with the addition of ripe wedges of tomatoes as a garnish and fresh peas, steamed until just tender and tossed with the other ingredients. Or spoon a little of the rice salad into small, crisp bibb lettuce leaves and arrange on a platter as a buffet dish.

WINE SUGGESTION: A light-bodied red wine, such as an Italian Bardolino.

1½ cups chicken stock (see page 198)	3 tablespoons parsley, chopped
½ cup white wine	1 chicken breast, split
2 tablespoons butter	Juice of 1 lemon
1 cup onions, chopped	Olive oil
1 cup long grain rice	Salt and pepper to taste
½ teaspoon saffron	

Bring stock and wine just to a boil, reduce heat, and keep at just below a simmer. While this is heating, melt butter, add chopped onions, and cook until soft. Add rice and stir to coat grains with butter. Pour in ¾ cup of the stock mixture, cover, and cook over low heat until liquid is absorbed. Add remaining stock in small increments, letting the rice absorb the liquid each time. Crumble saffron into the last bit of stock added. The rice should be stirred each time liquid is added, and recovered each time. It will take about 20 minutes for the entire process, at which time the rice should be tender but not overly soft. The entire dish will be a rich yellow from the saffron tendrils.

Stir the chopped parsley through the rice and let it cool while poaching chicken breasts and making the dressing. To poach the breasts, barely cover with water and bring to a boil. Reduce to a lively simmer, cover, and cook for 20 minutes. Remove chicken from the pot. When cool, skin, bone, and cut into dice.

Meanwhile, squeeze the juice of 1 lemon into a measuring cup, add olive oil to the ⅓-cup mark, and add salt and pepper to taste.

Stir chicken into rice, add the lemon-oil dressing, and toss thoroughly.

SERVES SIX AS A FIRST COURSE.

RICE SALAD II

The method for making this rice salad is similar to that of Rice Salad I, but the taste is entirely different, since the lemon juice, which is part of the stock in this version, gives it a decidedly piquant flavor. It can be tossed with cold crabmeat and a thin mayonnaise for a first course, but it would also make a nice summer luncheon salad, using seasonal fresh vegetables—such as steamed artichoke hearts, asparagus tips, and sprigs of watercress, instead of the crabmeat.

If used as a first course, it would be comfortably followed by broiled red snapper and a fresh spinach and mushroom salad. For dessert, cold zabaglione (see page 182).

WINE SUGGESTION: A full-bodied and elegant white burgundy-type wine, such as a French or American Chardonnay.

2 tablespoons butter	1 teaspoon salt
2 tablespoons shallots, chopped	1½ cups cold, cooked
1 cup long grain rice	crabmeat
1½ cups chicken stock	½ cup thin mayonnaise
½ cup lemon juice	

Melt the butter and add shallots, cooking only until the shallots are soft. Add rice and stir to coat grains. Meanwhile, heat the stock and lemon juice almost to the boiling point. Add about ¾ cup of the hot liquid to the rice, cover, and cook over low heat until liquid is absorbed. Continue adding the stock and lemon juice in small portions, stirring after each addition. Cover the rice each time and wait until the liquid has been absorbed before adding more, about 20 minutes in all.

When done, let cook to room temperature and toss with crabmeat and mayonnaise.

SERVES SIX AS A FIRST COURSE.

GOLDEN LEMON DUMPLINGS

The joy of these cloudlike mini dumplings is not only in the eating, but in the preparation. The mixture starts out as a *pâte à choux*—or traditional cream puff dough—but after being spooned into the bubbling stock, it puffs up into little feathery, free-form dumplings, wonderfully savory when served in a clear, rich soup as a first course. You can prepare them ahead, drain them, and reheat in simmering soup for a few minutes. The dumplings can also double as a garniture for meat or poultry in place of potatoes or other more usual starches.

To complete a meal that begins with the lemon dumplings in broth, follow with chicken breasts lightly sautéed with fresh mushrooms, strips of peeled eggplant, and a whisper of garlic. Serve a salad of curly chicory and sliced baby beets in a light vinaigrette. For dessert, cubes of fresh, peeled and cored pineapple marinated in a little Grand Marnier and served icy cold.

WINE SUGGESTIONS: A dry Fino sherry with the soup. A light, dry white wine, such as a Soave from Italy, with the chicken breasts.

3 large eggs, separated	1 cup sifted flour
⅓ cup lemon juice	4 tablespoons Romano
2 quarts rich chicken stock	cheese, freshly grated
(see page 198)	Freshly ground white
1 tablespoon butter	pepper to taste

Separate the eggs, dropping the whites into a 1-cup measuring glass. Add lemon juice and enough of the chicken stock to fill the measure to the 1-cup level. Place the remaining chicken stock in a large saucepan and bring slowly to a boil.

In a small saucepan melt the butter. Add the flour and egg-lemon-stock mixture all at once. With a wooden spoon or wire whisk stir over brisk heat for a few minutes, just until the mixture leaves the sides of the pan. Cool slightly. Add the grated cheese and the egg yolks, one at a time, beating well after each addition, until smooth. Mixture should be fairly thick.

Now, turn to the stock, which should be at a rolling boil. Form the dumplings, using a teaspoonful of batter for each, and drop them into the boiling stock. Depending on size, there should be 24 to 28. After they have risen to the top, lower heat and simmer for 10 minutes. Pour the dumplings and poaching stock into a soup tureen and serve at once. Or serve from the soup pot into heated soup bowls.

To serve them as an accompaniment to meat or poultry, re-move the dumplings from the stock with a slotted spoon after they have risen to the top and cooked for 10 minutes. Place them in a colander until thoroughly drained. Melt 3 tablespoons of butter in a heavy skillet or oven-proof casserole. Add the drained dumplings and simmer just until heated through, about 10 min-utes. Or they may be heated in a 350° F. oven, covered, for 10 to 15 minutes. Sprinkle finely minced fresh parsley over the dump-lings before serving.

SERVES FOUR TO SIX.

LEMON-CHEESE MERINGUES

These are actually a cross between a macaroon and an un-sweetened meringue. They're very easily made—ground almonds, Parmesan cheese, and grated lemon rind are folded into egg whites and baked in a low oven until light and crisp.

You can serve these tiny meringues with drinks or pass them as a special garnish with soup—perhaps a thin, rich tomato consommé. Follow with a filet of beef roast cooked to crispness outside and rare juiciness inside; mushrooms tossed in a skillet with lemon juice, butter, and shallots, then covered with heavy cream and cooked gently until the mushrooms have absorbed all the scented cream (see page 41); and tender, young asparagus tips, barely cooked. For dessert, scoops of vanilla ice cream with hot caramel sauce.

WINE SUGGESTION: A fine, mouth-filling Bordeaux, such as a Saint-Emilion or a California Pinot Noir.

> 3 tablespoons ground almonds
> 3 tablespoons Parmesan cheese, grated
> 2 teaspoons lemon rind, grated
> 2 egg whites

Preheat oven to 300° F.

The almonds and the Parmesan cheese should be almost the consistency of flour. Toss both with the grated lemon rind. With a wire whisk, beat the 2 egg whites until stiff. Fold the dry almond-Parmesan-lemon-rind mixture into the egg whites. Using 2 dessert spoons, drop the mixture onto a lightly buttered and floured cookie sheet. Bake in the preheated oven for 20 minutes. Turn heat off and leave the meringues in the oven with the door open until totally dry. If you are not going to eat them immediately, store in an airtight tin container. They should be feather-light and tenderly crisp.

MAKES ABOUT EIGHTEEN MERINGUES.

LEMON-PARMESAN BREAD

We find this a refreshing alternative to garlic bread. Grated Parmesan cheese, bits of lemon pulp, and generous amounts of butter are spread on halves of Italian whole-wheat bread, then run under the broiler.

Pile warm chunks of it in a basket and serve with drinks before dinner. Or it could accompany a first course of clams in a spicy tomato sauce and be followed by steamed whiting with chive butter. For dessert, a chocolate mousse.

> ¼ pound butter, softened
> 3 tablespoons Parmesan cheese, grated
> Pulp of 1 lemon
> 1 large loaf of Italian whole-wheat bread

Cream the butter with 2 tablespoons of the cheese. To obtain the lemon pulp, peel the lemon carefully, making sure the white pith is pared away. With a knife, slice each little lemon segment away from the core. Chop the lemon segments into small pieces and mix in with the butter and cheese.

Slice the bread horizontally so that you have 2 large halves. Spread with the butter mixture and sprinkle with the remaining tablespoon of cheese. Place under broiler until lightly browned. Cut into wedges.

SERVES EIGHT.

ENTREES

POACHED SALMON STEAKS WITH LEMON SAUCE

When salmon steaks are gently poached in an aromatic broth they become beautifully pink and succulent. Served with a velvet-textured lemon sauce, which, incidentally, uses no flour or cornstarch, they are elegant. As a perfect summer luncheon or supper entrée, the salmon fillets can be garnished with cherry tomatoes, thinly sliced cucumbers, and black olives and served with fresh asparagus for a profusion of colors, textures, and tastes. For dessert, a fresh peach torte.

WINE SUGGESTION: A well-chilled, bone-dry and elegant white wine, such as Chablis or Pouilly-Fuissé.

THE SALMON

4 fresh salmon steaks, each cut ½ inch thick
1 small onion, sliced
4 sprigs Italian parsley
⅛ teaspoon thyme
1 tiny piece of bay leaf, no larger than a thumbnail

Salt and freshly ground white pepper to taste
3 cups dry white wine
2 tablespoons lemon juice
Water

THE LEMON SAUCE

3 extra large or 4 large egg yolks	⅛ teaspoon salt
1 teaspoon sugar	A few shakes of cayenne pepper
½ cup lemon juice	1 tablespoon crème fraîche
½ cup reserved fish poaching liquid	(see page 200)

Use a fish poacher or a heavy skillet or Dutch oven large enough to hold the salmon steaks without crowding. Place the fish in the pan, add the onion, parsley, thyme, bay leaf, salt and freshly ground pepper, the wine, lemon juice, and enough water to cover the steaks completely. Bring to a boil, lower heat, and simmer for 5 minutes. Turn off the heat and permit the fish to cool in the liquid for a half-hour. Lift out the steaks carefully, using a flat, slotted spatula, and place them on a platter. Reserve the poaching liquid. Cool the salmon and strip off the skins. You may serve both the fish and the sauce at room temperature, if you wish. Otherwise, cover the salmon steaks with plastic wrap and re-frigerate until ready to serve.

To make the sauce, break the egg yolks into a metal bowl. (Save the whites for meringues.) Add the sugar and lemon juice and beat with a wire whisk until light. Place the bowl over sim-mering—never boiling—water and continue to beat for 5 minutes. Add the reserved fish poaching liquid gradually, and continue to beat over low heat until the mixture thickens slightly, about 15 minutes. The sauce should be the consistency of heavy cream. It will continue to thicken slightly as it cools. It will also thicken if covered and placed in the refrigerator. Correct seasoning with salt and cayenne pepper. Store, covered in the refrigerator until ready to serve.

To assemble for serving, transfer the fish steaks to a large, oval platter and garnish with cherry tomatoes, thinly sliced cucumbers, and black olives. Pass a sauceboat of lemon sauce and offer a platter of fresh asparagus, boiled briefly in a little water until crisp-tender and dressed with melted butter and lemon.

SERVES FOUR.

SOLE IN LEMON SAUCE

Lemon sole fillets are layered between chopped mushrooms and baked in a buttery lemon and wine sauce for a dish that is remarkably easy to prepare and serve.

A long, shallow baking dish will be perfect for this recipe because you will want to serve the sole from the dish in which it is baked. Have lots of fresh, unbuttered and untoasted French bread on hand, as there will be plenty of delicious sauce. Serve an avocado salad as a first course: fill avocado halves with vinaigrette and surround them with paper-thin slices of red onion and tomato wedges. For dessert, a coffee mousse topped with puffs of meringue.

WINE SUGGESTION: A crisp, assertive white wine, such as a California Fumé Blanc.

1 tablespoon olive oil
4 tablespoons butter
½ pound mushrooms, chopped
3 tablespoons shallots, minced

2¾ pounds lemon sole, filleted
½ cup dry white wine
⅓ cup lemon juice
½ teaspoon salt

Preheat oven to 350° F.

In a shallow baking dish, put the olive oil, 2 tablespoons of the butter and half the chopped mushrooms and shallots. Lay the fillets of sole on top of this with bits of the remaining 2 table-spoons of butter interspersed between the layers. Cover the sole with the remaining mushrooms and shallots. Pour wine and lemon juice, mixed, over all, add salt, and bake for 25 minutes.

SERVES FOUR.

RED SNAPPER WITH PUREED BROCCOLI

A smooth vegetable purée, judiciously seasoned, is a lovely addition to a meal. A purée can be used in many different ways, too —in freshly boiled artichoke bottoms or in a flaky barquette. In this recipe, the broccoli stems are blanched, then puréed with lemon juice, sautéed onions, and cheese, and served with the broccoli flowerets that have been tossed in butter.

The red snapper is broiled briefly with a liberal basting of melted butter and lemon juice and served on a platter with the purée in the center and the flowerets tucked around the purée.

A small antipasto—mushrooms, sliced cucumbers, and artichoke hearts with a simple oil and vinegar dressing—would make an interesting first course. For dessert, individual meringues with coffee ice cream and toffee sauce.

WINE SUGGESTIONS: A bone-dry white Chablis or a full-bodied, stylish white wine, such as a California Chardonnay.

THE BROCCOLI

> 2 pounds broccoli
> ¼ cup onions, chopped
> 3 tablespoons butter, melted
> ¼ cup lemon juice
> ⅓ cup Gruyère cheese, grated

THE FISH

> 2 tablespoons butter
> Juice of 2 lemons
> Red snapper, weighing 4½ pounds, then boned and filleted

Cut broccoli flowerets from stems and set aside. Cut rough edges from the base of the stems and chop stems into approximately 2-inch pieces. Bring 2 quarts of water to a boil, add stems, and boil gently for 10 to 15 minutes, or until stems can be pierced easily with the tines of a fork. Drain.

Next, cook chopped onions in 1 tablespoon of melted butter for 2 or 3 minutes or until just soft. Add lemon juice and cook for another 3 minutes so that the flavors meld. Put blanched broccoli stems, grated cheese, and the onion and lemon juice mixture into a blender and purée. Put the purée into saucepan and set aside until ready to use.

Bring another 2 quarts of water to a boil, or use the same liquid in which the stems were cooked. When water is at a high boil, add flowerets and continuing boiling for just 4 minutes. Drain and set aside.

The flowerets and the purée can be done several hours before serving. If you do them ahead of time, cover and refrigerate. Just before serving, heat the purée in a saucepan and toss flowerets in the remaining 2 tablespoons of melted butter. Cook only until heated through. Put purée in the center of a large platter, surrounded by the sautéed flowerets, and arrange the broiled red snapper fillets at either end of the platter.

To prepare the fish, melt butter in a small saucepan and add lemon juice. Place fillets, skin side down on a lightly oiled shallow pan, or on foil. Slide under broiler—fish should be 4 inches below flame—and broil according to the formula below. Baste every 3 minutes or so with the lemon-butter mixture. The cooking time will probably be quite brief; most red snapper fillets are about 1-inch thick, making the broiling time 8 to 10 minutes.

SERVES FOUR.

Note: A basic rule that is almost infallible for poaching, braising, or broiling fish is to cook the fish 10 minutes for every inch of thickness.

BAKED RED SNAPPER WITH LEMON-ONION SAUTE

The delicate flavor of the fresh red snapper is heightened by a gentle sauté of onions, lemons, and butter that is reduced to a glaze and perfumed with fresh herbs. Tiny new potatoes, boiled briefly in their jackets, are added to the pan in which the fish is baking during the last 20 minutes. French green beans, cooked until just crisp and served with melted butter, salt and freshly ground pepper, provide color and taste contrast.

A nice beginning would be sorrel soup (see page 18), served either chilled or hot, depending on the season. For dessert, crème brulée.

WINE SUGGESTION: An elegant, full-bodied, dry white wine, such as Puligny-Montrachet or California Chardonnay.

4 tablespoons butter	One 4-pound red snapper,
4 cups yellow onions, chopped	boned but left intact,
(about 3 large onions)	book-style
1 lemon, peeled, seeded, and	Salt and freshly ground
chopped	white pepper to taste
⅓ cup Italian parsley,	¾ cup dry white wine
finely chopped	8 scrubbed new potatoes,
2 to 3 sprigs fresh thyme or	skins on
⅛ teaspoon dried	1 tablespoon chives, thinly
	sliced

Preheat oven to 350° F.

In a large skillet melt the butter, add the chopped onions and chopped lemon, and sauté over a low flame for 5 to 8 minutes, until the mixture is thick and glazed. Add the chopped parsley and sprigs of thyme, stir, and take off heat.

Butter a large, oval baking dish and place the red snapper in the center. Sprinkle fish with salt and pepper inside and out. Stuff with the onion-lemon mixture. Pour the white wine over the fish and bake in the preheated oven for 20 minutes, basting from time to time with the pan juices. After 20 minutes, add parboiled new potatoes and continue to bake until the fish is done, another 15 to 20 minutes.

Place the baked fish on a heated, heavy serving platter. Criss-cross spikes of chives on top of the fish, encircle with the new potatoes, and serve at once.

SERVES FOUR.

GOUJONETTES OF SOLE
(Deep-Fried Strips of Sole)

Goujons are tiny French river fish, delectable when fried whole and eaten in one crisp crunch. Since we don't have goujons here, the next best thing is to cut fillets of sole into small strips and deep fry the strips until golden—and call them goujonettes which means in the style of goujon. We use lemon sole, which is really a big, beautiful flounder, boned and filleted, lightly coated with lemon zest and bread crumbs ground as powdery as flour. The flounder, being a little heavier than grey or Dover sole, makes goujonettes that are moist and succulent inside. If you slice the fish into very slim goujonettes, they make marvelous companions to apéritifs. For an entrée you can slice the fillets into more substantial 2-by-2-inch squares. Serve them with a bowl of homemade tartar sauce, fresh green peas steamed in lettuce leaves, and a salad of tomato slices and Jerusalem artichokes in a light vinaigrette. For dessert, angel cake layered with whipped cream and sliced fresh strawberries.

WINE SUGGESTION: A crisp, bone-dry white wine, such as Muscadet from the Loire Valley in France or a California Fumé Blanc.

2 pounds lemon sole fillets
1 egg beaten with 1 tablespoon of water

1½ cups homemade bread crumbs, very finely pulverized

Zest of 2 large lemons, very
  finely grated
Salt and freshly ground
  white pepper to taste

Oil for deep frying
Parsley heads for garnish

Wipe the fillets and cut them into 2-by-2-inch squares or in ¾-inch strips. Beat the egg and water until well mixed and place the mixture in a shallow dish. Mix the fine bread crumbs with the grated lemon zest and place in a shallow plate. Dip the fish strips first in the beaten egg, then the bread-crumb-lemon-zest mixture so they're lightly coated on both sides.

Fill a heavy, cast-iron skillet or a French fry pan with light frying oil to a depth of about 2 inches. Heat the oil to the sizzling point, or until a small bit of bread dropped into it turns golden very quickly. Slide in the fish fillets, as many as will fit your pan comfortably, and fry for several minutes on each side, or until golden. Remove with a slotted spatula or spoon and drain on paper towels. Transfer to a heated platter, garnish with a few parsley leaves, and serve with a bowl of tartar sauce (recipe follows).

SERVES FOUR.

Note: If you own a Cuisinart or other food processor, you may place strips of lemon zest in the container along with the bread cubes and process them together.

TARTAR SAUCE
2 egg yolks
1 tablespoon cider vinegar
½ teaspoon dry or 1 teaspoon
  Dijon mustard
¼ teaspoon each salt and white
  pepper
1 cup salad oil

2 tablespoons lemon juice
2 tablespoons green olives,
  finely minced
2 tablespoons capers, drained
2 tablespoons cornichons or
  gherkins, finely minced
1 teaspoon cold water

Combine egg yolks, vinegar, mustard, salt and pepper in the container of a blender or food processor. Blend briefly. Slowly add the salad oil, scraping down the sides of the container to blend evenly. When all the oil has been used, the mixture should be thick and creamy. Add the lemon juice, olives, capers, cornichons, and the water, which helps to stabilize the sauce, and stir just to mix. If it seems too thick, add a little more lemon juice. Pour into a jar with a tight lid. It will keep up to a week in the refrigerator.

MAKES APPROXIMATELY ONE CUP.

SWORDFISH BAKED WITH DILL SAUCE

A kingly fish is the swordfish, with its firm white flesh and unique superb flavor. Broiled swordfish tends to be dry even when butter-basted, so baking is the best choice. The fish is first marinated in lemon juice and freshly ground pepper, then baked and sauced with a refreshing blend of sour cream, snipped dill, and a hint of mint. It makes an elegant entrée, accompanied by tiny, buttered potato balls and whole tender young green beans, cooked until just crunchy-crisp. To start, serve a cluster of littleneck clams nestling on a bed of crushed ice with nothing more to hide their nakedness than a squirt of lemon juice. For dessert, a blackberry trifle.

WINE SUGGESTION: An elegant and full-bodied white wine, such as Pouilly-Fuissé or a California Chardonnay.

THE FISH

4 individual swordfish steaks, 1-inch thick
Salt and freshly ground white pepper to taste

Juice of 1 lemon
4 tablespoons sweet butter

THE DILL SAUCE
Mix together in a bowl:

¼ cup lemon juice
1 cup dairy sour cream
4 tablespoons fresh dill, finely chopped
2 tablespoons onion, grated
1 teaspoon fresh mint leaves, finely chopped, or a dash of
    mint extract
Salt and white pepper to taste

Preheat oven to 425° F.

Place fish steaks in a dish that will accommodate them in one layer. Grind white pepper over the surfaces on both sides, and add salt. Pour the juice of a lemon over the steaks and let them marinate for at least a half-hour at room temperature, turning once. (In summer, marinate steaks in the refrigerator.)

Transfer fish steaks to a lightly buttered baking dish that will hold them comfortably. Pour marinade over the steaks. Place 1 tablespoon of butter on each steak and bake for 20 minutes, or until tender when pronged with the tines of a fork. Baste the steaks with the pan juices once or twice during baking because swordfish has a tendency to dry out.

Remove the baking dish from the oven, but leave the oven on. Using a large spoon or basting bulb, carefully remove accumulated juices. (You may discard these juices or save them to enrich a fish soup, in which case, pour them into a lidded jar and refrigerate.) Spoon the dill sauce on the fish steaks, spreading the mixture evenly to cover the tops completely. Return the fish to the oven and bake another 6 to 7 minutes, or just until the topping has set. The dill sauce need not brown. It must, however, be firm enough to remain on top of the fish without sliding off when the baking dish is gently joggled. Serve at once.

SERVES FOUR.

Note: Halibut steaks may be prepared in the same manner. Again, check for doneness with the tines of a fork.

STRIPED BASS JARDINIERE

Papery slices of sweet red onion and little golden circles of lemon are interleaved with red-ripe tomatoes flecked with chopped fresh basil and Italian parsley, drizzled with fine Italian olive oil, and are placed both inside and on top of a fresh, boned striped bass. The fish is given a generous splash of dry white wine, then baked until the flesh is opaque and the seasoned mélange of vegetables and fish juices forms a fragrant sauce. Bake the fish in a handsome ovenproof dish that you can bring to the table. A bowl of rice cooked in broth and a little oil until each grain glistens, and a basket of crusty Italian whole wheat bread would go well with it.

The meal starts with a thin, rich cream of carrot soup. For dessert, scoops of vanilla ice cream with a sauce of fresh strawberries puréed with a little sugar.

WINE SUGGESTION: A bone-dry, crisp white wine, such as a California Fumé Blanc or Pouilly Fumé from France's Loire Valley.

One 4-pound striped bass,
boned, but left open like a
book

1 cup sweet red Bermuda
onions, sliced as thinly as
possible

2 small lemons, sliced as thinly
as possible

3 medium-sized red-ripe
tomatoes, peeled and
thinly sliced

½ cup Italian parsley,
leaves only, finely
minced

¼ cup fresh basil, finely
chopped, or 1 teaspoon
dried

Salt and freshly ground
white pepper to taste

¼ cup fine Italian olive oil

1 cup dry white wine or
dry vermouth

Preheat oven to 375° F.

Have the fish man bone the striped bass but leave the fish whole so that it may be stuffed. Place fish in a lightly oiled ovenproof baking dish. Open the fish and layer with half the onions, lemons, tomatoes, the fresh parsley and basil. Add salt and freshly ground pepper and drizzle with half the oil. Close the fish and cover with the remaining vegetables, herbs, and lemon. Drizzle on the remaining oil and pour dry white wine or vermouth over all.

Bake in the preheated oven for 25 to 30 minutes, basting several times with the pan juices.

SERVES FOUR.

SCALLOPS IN COGNAC BROTH

Tiny bay scallops are simmered briefly in a butter sauce livened with Cognac, minced fresh ginger root, and lemon juice just long enough for the scallops to render their natural sweet juices. The sauce is reduced to thicken it slightly and permit the flavors to coalesce.

We like to serve this dish in deep Italianate soup bowls, with lots of crusty Italian whole-wheat bread. Accompany this light supper entrée with bottles of chilled light, crisp Italian white wine. For dessert, a basket of crisp apples and pears and wedges of Bel Paese and Gorgonzola cheeses.

WINE SUGGESTION: A chilled Italian white wine, such as Verdicchio from central Italy or a white Corvo from Sicily.

¼ pound sweet butter	2 tablespoons fresh ginger
1 cup Cognac	root, finely minced
½ cup lemon juice	¼ cup Italian parsley,
1 teaspoon salt	finely minced
	2 pounds bay scallops

Melt the butter in a large skillet over low heat. Add Cognac, lemon juice, salt, ginger root, parsley and simmer for 5 minutes, stirring to prevent burning. Place the bay scallops in the skillet and simmer for 5 minutes, stirring once or twice. Remove scallops with a slotted spoon to a heatproof bowl and keep warm. Turn heat to medium and reduce the sauce, stirring, for 5 to 6 minutes. Pour it over the scallops and ladle into hot soup bowls to be served at once.

SERVES FOUR.

MUSSELS IN LEMON-CREAM SAUCE

Plump, pink mussels lend themselves to a variety of interesting preparations, and it's the ingredients used in the steaming of these black-shelled mollusks that make the difference in the final sauce.

In this recipe, butter, lemon juice, wine, a little garlic, and minced onion mix with the sea-flavored juices exuded by the mussels. The stock is reduced, heavy cream is added, and the mussels then immersed in this flavorsome sauce.

Serve the mussels in bowls, accompanied with Italian whole-wheat bread that has been toasted and slathered with butter. A hearty Caesar salad could follow the mussels. For dessert, a fresh peach cobbler.

WINE SUGGESTION: A crisp, dry white wine, such as a Muscadet from France's Loire Valley.

8 pounds mussels	1 small onion, minced
6 tablespoons butter	1 clove garlic, minced
1 cup dry white wine	2 tablespoons flour
½ cup lemon juice	½ cup heavy cream

Wash mussels under cold water, scrubbing the shells well and pulling off the beards—the seaweed-like tendrils that trail out of the shells.

Place cleaned mussels in a deep stock pot and add 4 tablespoons of the butter, the wine, lemon juice, onion, and garlic. Cover the pot, bring the mixture to a boil, and steam mussels for about 7 minutes, or until the shells are open.

Pour mussels into a colander that has been set over a bowl to catch the cooking liquid. Discard any mussels with shells that have not opened. Remove mussels from shells and set aside.

Strain the mussel liquid through cheesecloth into a saucepan, bring to a boil, and cook over medium heat until reduced to 1½ cups.

In a large skillet or pan, melt the remaining 2 tablespoons of butter. Add flour and stir until mixture is smooth. Bring to a bubbling stage and let cook, stirring constantly, for 1 minute. Remove from heat, and when bubbling has subsided, add hot stock, whisking briskly. Continue whisking for a few seconds, then add cream. Stir well, add mussels, return to heat, and continue cooking only until the mussels are warmed through.

SERVES FOUR.

BRANDADE DE MORUE
(Salt Cod Puréed with Garlic, Cream, and Oil)

The origin of this creamy puréed cod, fragrant with garlic, is Provence. It is traditionally served with triangles of fried bread but is also good with baked or boiled potatoes and a leafy salad.

Although the dried cod must be soaked for 24 hours, during which it will almost double in size, the dish itself is relatively easy to prepare if you have a blender or food processor.

For dessert, pear sorbet.

WINE SUGGESTION: A steely dry white wine, such as Sancerre from the Loire Valley in France, or a California Sauvignon Blanc, sometimes called Fumé Blanc.

> 1 pound dried salt cod
> 2 cloves garlic, minced
> 1⅓ cups olive oil

1¼ cups heavy cream
4 tablespoons lemon juice

Soak the cod in cold water for at least 24 hours, changing the water occasionally. Drain and place the cod in a saucepan with enough water to just cover and bring slowly to a near simmer— the water on top should be moving slightly but not bubbling. Maintain at this point for 10 minutes. Drain cod and pat dry.

Place cod, garlic, olive oil, and 1 cup of the cream in a blender and purée. Pour the mixture into a saucepan and heat, beating in the remaining ¼ cup cream and lemon juice. When hot and smooth, mound the brandade on a platter and garnish with watercress and wedges of ripe tomatoes.

SERVES FOUR AS A MAIN COURSE.

VEGETABLE TEMPURA

Although the Japanese tempura traditionally applies to batter-dipped, deep-fried shrimps, we like to use the tempura batter for vegetables. The addition of icy-cold fresh lemon juice to the batter is sensational, imparting just the right degree of tartness and delicacy. When the vegetables are dipped into the batter, then plunged briefly into a hot oil bath, they emerge encased in golden, crisp little shells that are utterly irresistible. They must be served almost at once, for standing too long robs them of their crispness. We use thinly sliced zucchini, tiny cauliflowerets, and asparagus cut into one-inch pieces, but you can use almost any fresh vegetable and, of course, shrimps, if you desire.

Serve with a little bowl of dipping sauce and a large bowl of fluffy steamed rice. Bowls of clear Japanese-style soup—rich beef stock garnished with slivers of green onions and a slice of raw mushroom—would be delightful before the tempura. For dessert, something simple, fresh pineapple or lichee nuts.

WINE SUGGESTION: Warmed rice wine, such as sake, served in tiny cups.

THE BATTER

> 1 egg
> ⅔ cup lemon juice, well chilled
> 1 cup flour, sifted twice
> A pinch of baking soda

THE VEGETABLES

> 2 large zucchini, sliced
> 1 small white cauliflower
> 12 fresh, fat asparagus spears
> Oil for frying

To make the batter, break the egg into a mixing bowl and beat with a wire whisk until light. Gradually add the cold lemon juice, beating until blended. Then slowly add the sifted flour and baking soda, beating with the whisk until thoroughly combined. The batter should be fairly thick, like pancake batter.

Wash, dry, and trim the ends off the zucchini. Cut into thin rounds. Let stand on paper towels for 10 minutes to absorb moisture.

Wash, dry, and trim the cauliflower and break or cut into tiny flowerets. Peel asparagus with a vegetable peeler and cut into 1-inch pieces.

To deep fry, use a deep fry pan or any large skillet that will hold about 3 inches of oil. Heat the salad oil to 375° F. on a deep-fry thermometer. If you don't have a thermometer, the oil will be hot enough to fry when a tiny piece of bread sizzles immediately when dropped into the pan.

When the oil is ready, dip the vegetables into the batter, using a long-handled fork or spoon. See that each piece is entirely coated with batter. Drop the pieces into hot oil and cook, turning each piece once with a long-handled spoon, until golden. This will take 1 or 2 minutes. Remove with a long-handled slotted spoon and drain on paper towels. Keep the finished vegetables warm by placing them in a 300° F. oven until you've finished frying them all. Serve as soon as possible.

SERVES THREE.

THE DIPPING SAUCE
½ cup light soy sauce
½ cup dry white wine
½ to 1 teaspoon fresh ginger root, finely grated, depending on the degree of hotness you like. If fresh ginger root is not available, substitute ½ teaspoon powdered ginger

Combine all ingredients in a small bowl, stirring to blend well.

POULET AU CITRON
(Lemon Chicken)

This dish can be made quickly and takes advantage of the wonderful affinity that butter, lemon, cheese, and chicken have for one another. The boned chicken breasts are poached gently in butter, surrounded by lemon slices, and, just before serving, are covered with Emmenthal cheese, which then melts over the chicken and lemon. A moist, saffron-flavored risotto goes well with this, along with a salad of romaine and raw mushrooms in a mustard vinaigrette. For dessert, crème caramel.

WINE SUGGESTION: A fruity, somewhat robust white wine from Burgundy, such as a Mâcon Blanc or Saint Véran.

> 4 tablespoons butter
> 2 lemons
> 4 chicken breasts, boned, skinned, and split
> ¼ pound Emmenthal or Gruyère cheese

Preheat oven to 350° F.

Cut 1 whole lemon and half of the other lemon into thin slices, and strew in the bottom of a baking dish. Add butter and heat over low flame until butter is melted. Remove from heat and place chicken breasts, which have been folded under to form tidy mounds, on top of the lemon slices. Squeeze juice from the remaining lemon half over the chicken. Bake, uncovered, in the preheated oven for 20 minutes, basting once or twice. Meanwhile, slice the cheese into small, thin pieces. When the 20 minutes are up, remove the chicken from the oven and place the cheese on top of the chicken breasts. Return to the oven for 5 minutes, or until the cheese has started to melt and coats the chicken breasts.

SERVES FOUR.

PETITES POCHES
(Stuffed Chicken Breasts)

The little pockets that are formed when the skin on boned chicken breasts is loosened from the meat lend themselves to a variety of delicious stuffings—in this case, a sauté of garlic and chopped lemon, stirred into ricotta cheese. Stuffed with this mixture, sautéed briefly, then baked, the breasts and their filling seem to melt together and are moist with a delicate flavor.

Serve them with braised endive and boiled new potatoes tossed with sweet butter and chopped parsley. For dessert, a mocha torte filled with coffee butter cream.

WINE SUGGESTION: A dry, full-bodied white wine, such as a French Mâcon Blanc or California Chardonnay.

4 tablespoons butter	4 large chicken breasts,
2 lemons, chopped	boned, but with the
2 cloves garlic, minced	skin left intact
1 teaspoon salt	3 tablespoons dry white
1½ to 2 cups ricotta cheese	wine

Preheat oven to 350° F.

Melt 2 tablespoons of the butter in a skillet. Add the lemons, which have been chopped with the skin left on, and the garlic. Sprinkle salt over the mixture and sauté gently until the lemon, its juices, and the butter have cooked together and become slightly thick. Remove from heat and combine the garlic-lemon mixture with the ricotta cheese, mixing well.

Meanwhile, place chicken breasts on a platter or on waxed paper. Trim any extra globules of fat that hang over the edges. Then, with your fingers, gently loosen the skin on each breast from the meat, trying to keep the skin and meat attached around the edges. The object is to make a pocket into which you will place the ricotta filling. You may have to use scissors to cut the center tissue which acts like a little seam between the skin and the meat. If the skin happens to pull away at the edge, it doesn't matter, since chicken skin is quite pliable and can be stretched out and under the chicken breast to hold the stuffing in place.

Once the skins have been loosened and you have a nice hollow space, fill it with the ricotta mixture, using either a spoon, your fingers, or both. Next, tuck the edges of the breast under so that you have 4 puffy mounds. Melt the remaining 2 tablespoons of butter in a baking dish large enough to accommodate the 4 breasts. Place the breasts, underside down, into the hot butter and cook briefly, for about 2 minutes. Turn them so that the stuffed side is in the hot butter and sauté until brown, about 5 minutes. Place them right side up, add white wine to the butter, and put in the preheated oven for 25 minutes, basting once or twice.

SERVES FOUR.

CHICKEN BREASTS FIORENTINA

Fiorentina, or Florentine, usually means something served on a bed of spinach, but here chicken breasts are served under a coverlet of spinach. The breasts are baked, covered with a mixture of finely minced spinach leaves, sweet butter, lemon juice, and freshly grated Parmesan cheese, then run under the broiler for a few minutes until the topping is set. A pretty garniture is saffron-tinted rice and cherry tomatoes braised briefly in butter, salt, and pepper. Start the meal with a cup of fragrant vegetable soup. For dessert, a fresh plum tart.

WINE SUGGESTION: A light-bodied, dry white Italian wine, such as Verdicchio or Soave.

2 large chicken breasts, boned, skinned, and halved	½ pound fresh spinach leaves
Salt and freshly ground pepper to taste	3 tablespoons sweet butter, melted
½ cup dry white wine	¼ cup Parmesan cheese, finely grated
	3 tablespoons lemon juice

Preheat the oven to 350° F.

Wash and pat dry the chicken breasts and place them in an oven-proof dish. Sprinkle with salt and pepper and pour the white wine over them. Cover loosely with a length of aluminum foil and bake for 20 minutes. While they are baking, prepare the topping: wash the spinach leaves, remove stems and large veins, and pat dry with paper towels. Place the leaves in the container of a blender or food processor and process until they are the consistency of minced parsley. Turn the minced spinach into a bowl. Add the melted butter, finely grated Parmesan cheese, lemon juice, and a little freshly ground pepper. Mix with a wooden spoon or spatula until smooth and of a pastelike consistency.

When the breasts have baked 20 minutes, remove them from the oven, but leave them in the baking dish. Preheat the broiler.

Using a large spoon or spatula, spread enough of the spinach mixture over the tops to cover each completely. Place the dish under the broiler, about 3 inches from the heat, and broil for about 5 minutes, or until the topping is set.

SERVES TWO

CHICKEN ALLA FROIO
(Chicken with Lemon-Oil Sauce)

This is a delicious Italian lemon chicken, baked first, then crisped under the broiler, with a heady topping of lemon juice, garlic, olive oil, and parsley. The dish may be made with a whole chicken cut into serving pieces, or with whichever parts of the chicken you prefer—breasts, wings, thighs. The pungent chicken can be accompanied by a light risotto and braised escarole. As a first course, serve mussels vinaigrette. For dessert, a bowl of fresh seasonal apples and pears and wedges of Gorgonzola or other blue-veined cheeses.

WINE SUGGESTION: A light, red Bardolino or Valpolicella.

One 2½- to 3-pound chicken
  cut into serving pieces
Salt and freshly ground pepper
  to taste
½ teaspoon dried oregano or
  other preferred herb
3 tablespoons olive oil

3 tablespoons white wine
  vinegar
⅓ cup lemon juice
¼ cup olive oil
1 large clove garlic, finely
  minced
½ cup Italian parsley,
  coarsely chopped

Preheat oven to 350° F.

Place chicken pieces skin side up in a baking pan. Season with salt, pepper, and oregano, drizzle with 3 tablespoons olive oil and the wine vinegar. Cover the pan with aluminum foil and allow the chicken to marinate for at least a half-hour. Then bake the chicken, with a foil covering, for 45 to 50 minutes, depending on the size of the chicken.

Meanwhile, in a small bowl, mix together the lemon juice, ¼ cup olive oil, minced garlic, and chopped parsley. Beat the mixture with a fork or whisk until foamy. When the chicken is done, take it out of the oven, remove the foil, and turn the pieces skin side down. Run them under the broiler for a few minutes until crisp, turn again, and crisp the skin side under the broiler. Spoon the lemon-parsley mixture over the skin side of the chicken pieces and place under the broiler once again for 1 or 2 minutes.

SERVES TWO TO THREE.

One or two thoughts: The proportion of lemon to oil in the final step can be changed to suit one's taste; if a more lemony taste is desired, simply increase the amount of lemon juice. Also, before putting this final topping on the chicken, be sure that there is not an excess of pan juices; pour some off if it looks like too much or else the lemony mixture will be too diluted.

POULET A L'INDIENNE
(Spicy Chicken Breasts)

A fragrant mélange of spices and tiny julienne slices of lemon keep company overnight with boned chicken breasts in this recipe. The next day, all of it is simmered in a purée of onions and parsley. The result is gently exotic. Serve these chicken breasts with the most simple of accompaniments—boiled new potatoes, peeled and dressed only with butter and pepper, and an endive salad with vinaigrette. For dessert, something cool and sharp like lemon granita (see page 175) would be perfect.

WINE SUGGESTION: A well-chilled white wine with character, such as a spicy California or Alsatian Gewürztraminer.

Peel of 1 lemon, cut into small slivers
2 cloves garlic, minced
1 teaspoon ground ginger
1 teaspoon turmeric
¼ teaspoon green peppercorns, optional
1 teaspoon salt
3 tablespoons olive oil
1 tablespoon water
4 chicken breasts, split, boned, and skinned
1 cup parsley, chopped
2½ cups onion, chopped
Chicken stock
¼ teaspoon saffron
3 tablespoons butter

Combine the lemon peel, garlic, ginger, turmeric, peppercorns, salt, olive oil, and water in a container that will also accommodate the 8 chicken pieces. Mix these to a paste. Pat split chicken breasts dry and place in the spice mixture, turning the chicken to make sure the paste coats each piece well. Cover and refrigerate overnight, or for a day. The chicken should have at least 8 hours to get together with the spice marinade. When ready to complete the dish, purée the parsley and onion in a blender or food processor. Place the marinated chicken breasts in a heavy skillet. Add the puréed parsley and onion and enough chicken stock barely to cover. Add the saffron, which has been softened in a little hot water, and dot the breasts with the butter. Cover tightly and simmer until tender, about 30 minutes.

SERVES FOUR.

TAJINE DE POULET
(Moroccan-Style Chicken)

In Morocco, the word *tajine,* literally a pyramid-shaped pottery cooking pot, is also used to designate a stew of either chicken or meat, which is simmered together with onions and spices for a long time. The colorfully decorated pottery tajines are made to withstand and hold heat. After the dish is completed, the stew is served right from the tajine, usually accompanied by a native unleavened bread.

This recipe is an adaptation by Peter Davis Dibble of one of many authentic versions and is piquant and well seasoned but not overpowering. It makes a lovely entrée, especially for a dinner party, and may be prepared a day or even two days in advance, giving the flavors an opportunity to meld and intensify.

For a buffet party you might cube the chicken breasts into bite-sized pieces so that diners need not use a knife. Serve hot steamed rice, and Middle-Eastern flat pita bread, which is sold in many supermarkets or serve soft-crusted rolls, warmed in the oven. Follow with a crisp salad of bibb lettuce, fresh young spinach leaves, and sliced endive dressed with yogurt thinned with a bit of lemon juice and seasoned with salt and freshly ground pepper. For dessert, orange sherbet.

WINE SUGGESTION: Nothing subtle or it will be overwhelmed by the spices. A fruity, not-too-dry white wine, such as a Vouvray from the Loire Valley in France would be agreeable.

8 whole chicken breasts, halved	Freshly ground pepper to
¼ cup olive oil (more, if	taste
needed)	1½ cups water (more, if
1½ cups onions, minced	needed)
1 tablespoon sweet Spanish	4 to 6 lemons, quartered
paprika	and seeded
1½ teaspoons ground ginger	48 small, pitted green olives
½ teaspoon turmeric	Salt to taste

In a large skillet, brown the chicken on all sides in olive oil over moderately high heat. Transfer with a slotted spoon to a warm dish.

In the same skillet, sauté the minced onions until they are softened. Stir in the paprika, ginger, turmeric, and pepper to taste. Sauté the mixture 1 minute.

Reduce heat to moderate and add the water, stirring in any brown bits clinging to the bottom and sides of the skillet. Add the lemons and the chicken. Bring the liquid to a boil and simmer the mixture, covered, for 30 minutes, or until the chicken is tender.

Add the olives and simmer again for 5 minutes more. Transfer the chicken and lemons to a heated (preferably earthenware) casserole and keep warm.

Bring the sauce to a boil, cook until it has reduced and thickened, and add salt to taste. Pour the sauce over the chicken.
SERVES EIGHT.

CHICKEN CURRY

A good curry, served with a galaxy of condiments, can be a most festive meal.

The condiments can be served in individual lacquer dishes and arranged on a tray, or they can be mounded side-by-side on a large, shallow dish. Each individual chooses those he wants to add texture and taste to the curry, thus lending a certain element of surprise to the dish.

Our curry can be made ahead of time, the chicken poached and set aside, and the whole thing assembled and warmed at the last minute. In fact, we poach the chicken first, remove the meat from the bones, and return the bones to the liquid to cook into a nice stock which we then use to make the curry.

Depending on the number and type of condiments you choose to serve, any additional dish could be superfluous. However, if you want to serve a salad, sliced green apples, chopped scallions, and endive are a good combination with curry. For dessert, something soothing like a fruit ice or vanilla ice cream with a berry sauce.

WINE SUGGESTION: A well-chilled beer is the best cooling complement to a curry, but if you prefer wine, a moderately dry white, such as a California Mountain Chablis, served well chilled, is congenial.

3 tablespoons olive oil
1 large onion, coarsely chopped
2 tablespoons flour
2 tablespoons curry powder
3 cups chicken broth, warmed
¼ cup lemon juice
½ cup raw carrots, cut into
    julienne strips

⅔ cup apples, peeled and
    cut into julienne strips
1 tablespoon chutney
2 pounds chicken breasts,
    poached and cut into
    chunks

Warm the olive oil in a large skillet or sauté pan. Add onion, toss and cook until just limp. Sprinkle flour and curry powder over onion and stir. Add warmed chicken broth, 1 cup at a time, stirring after each addition, then the lemon juice. Stir and bring the mixture to a boil. Next, add carrots, apples, and chutney. Reduce heat and simmer the curry for 30 minutes. When ready to serve, add the poached chicken chunks and heat through. Serve over steamed rice.

SERVES FOUR.

SOME CONDIMENT SUGGESTIONS FOR FOUR:

1 large or 2 small green
    peppers, diced
3 large, hard-boiled eggs, the
    whites chopped and the
    yolks crumbled
1 cup chutney
1 cup preserved kumquats
6 slices bacon, fried and
    minced
4 scallions, minced

1 cup cashews, coarsely
    chopped
2 ripe bananas, thinly sliced
¾ cup parsley, minced
¾ cup crystallized ginger,
    diced
1½ cups tomatoes, skinned
    and chopped
1 cup fresh pineapple, diced

Note: Obviously, it is not necessary to serve 12 condiments, although it is very entertaining. However, you should always pro-

vide a chutney, some kind of chopped nut, one diced raw vegetable, and something bland, such as the chopped egg whites or a
cooling yogurt.

CAPON ROASTED WITH LEMON SLICES
UNDER THE SKIN

Capons are great, meaty birds that taste wonderful when roasted
this simple way. The chicken is basted by the lemon slices tucked
underneath the skin and with a combination of melted butter and
Madeira until it's invitingly golden and the lemon slices turn a
marvelous burnished color. Serve a creamy risotto and Italian
green beans sautéed in a little butter and chopped shallots with
the capon. Start off with a purée of fresh watercress soup enriched with a little heavy cream. For dessert, an apricot tart
warmed briefly in the oven.

WINE SUGGESTION: A big, full-bodied dry white wine, such as a
California Chardonnay or a Burgundian Puligny-Montrachet.

One 4½-pound capon or
   roasting chicken
Salt and freshly ground pepper
2 large lemons, thinly sliced
1 large onion
6 sprigs fresh tarragon or
   ¼ teaspoon dried

6 sprigs Italian parsley
4 tablespoons butter, melted
   and combined with
½ cup dry Madeira (Sercial
   or Rainwater)

Preheat oven to 350° F.

Wipe chicken dry and season inside and out with salt and pepper. Using a sharp knife, cut the skin around the breast and back, lifting it gently. Insert the slices of lemon at random, making certain the slices lay flat against the bird. Make slits with the knife at the top of the drumsticks and insert 1 or 2 lemon slices under the skin of each. Don't crowd the slices. There should be an inch or so of space between them. A random pattern will result in a beautiful bird. Place the onion, tarragon, and parsley in the cavity, truss or use skewers to hold the chicken in shape, and place it on a rack in a roasting pan, breast side down. Roast in the preheated oven for 35 minutes, basting once or twice with the melted butter-Madeira mixture. Turn the bird breast side up, baste again with the butter-Madeira, and roast an additional 60 to 65 minutes, or until the chicken is golden and the outline of the lemons burnished. (Chicken is done when the leg juices run clear yellow when pierced with the tines of a fork.) Transfer chicken to a heated platter. Remove onion and parsley and carve at table.

SERVES SIX.

GREAT GOLDEN GOOSE

When the goose hangs high it's a festive occasion. This bird, traditional for the Yuletide season in England and middle Europe, is great on any occasion, although its dark, meaty flesh and rich flavor make it especially appropriate during the brisk fall and frigid winter seasons.

The natural fatness of the goose is offset by rubbing it generously inside and out with cut lemons, adding lemon pulp to the stuffing, and basting the bird with lemon juice and Madeira. As it roasts, it literally turns golden. Accompany the goose with puréed celery root and tiny fresh peas cooked with finely shredded lettuce. With apéritifs, serve a platter of thinly sliced Scotch salmon. For dessert, Tarte Citron Mama (see page 163).

WINE SUGGESTION: A full-bodied red wine from Burgundy, such as a Côtes de Beaune-Villages, or a California Pinot Noir.

One 8-to-10-pound goose	1 cup golden raisins
Salt and freshly ground pepper	1 cup Italian parsley, leaves only, chopped
2 lemons, cut into halves	½ teaspoon each, marjoram, thyme, chervil, and sage
1 medium-sized head fresh green cabbage, very finely shredded	¼ teaspoon cracked allspice
6 firm, tart apples, peeled, cored, and coarsely chopped	1 cup dry white wine
1 lemon, peeled, seeded, and the pulp chopped	¾ cup Madeira (Sercial or Rainwater) combined with ½ cup lemon juice

The secret to ridding the goose of its fat is to roast it for an hour in a hot oven before stuffing it. The initial exposure to the hot oven will melt away a good deal of fat, which then can be discarded.

Preheat oven to 475° F.

Season the goose liberally with salt and freshly ground pepper and rub generously inside and out with cut lemon. Using the sharp tines of a carving fork, prick the bird all over, especially around the breast and thighs where fatty deposits lie. Place the goose on a rack in a large roasting pan and roast in the preheated oven for 1 hour. Remove the goose from the oven, lower the temperature to 350° F., pour off accumulated fat, and permit the bird to cool slightly. To stuff the goose, blanch shredded cabbage in a large pot of rapidly boiling water for 2 minutes. Drain and place it in a large bowl. Add the chopped apples, lemon pulp, and raisins and toss lightly. To this mixture add parsley, herbs, allspice, dry white wine, salt and freshly ground pepper, and toss everything together. Stuff the cavity of the goose lightly, truss, and place it back on the rack of the roasting pan.

Roast the goose 20 minutes to the pound. Draw off accumulated fat from time to time. Baste the goose periodically with the Madeira and lemon juice. It is done when the color is golden brown and the leg juices run clear yellow when pricked with the tines of a fork.

SERVES TEN.

CHICKEN LIVERS IN LEMON-WINE SAUCE

We like to have in our minds several recipes for those times when one wants a delicious little meal for two that doesn't require a lot of preparation. This is one of them. The livers are sautéed briefly. The wine and lemon juice are reduced, then thickened with butter and poured over the chicken livers. Crisp pieces of bacon garnish the dish. Toss endive and sprigs of watercress in a mustard vinaigrette as an accompanying salad. For dessert, a runny Brie with chunks of warmed French bread and a basket of tangerines.

WINE SUGGESTION: A light and fruity red wine, such as a Beaujolais or California Gamay Beaujolais, served slightly chilled.

5 tablespoons butter	¼ teaspoon tarragon
1 pound chicken livers	¼ teaspoon salt
¾ cup red Burgundy wine	4 slices bacon
¼ cup lemon juice	

Melt 2 tablespoons of the butter in a pan and sauté the chicken livers until they just lose their color. Remove with a slotted spoon and put them temporarily in a bowl. Add wine, lemon juice, tarragon, and salt and bring to a boil. Continue boiling until the liquid has reduced.

Meanwhile, as the livers exude their own juices, pour them into the wine-lemon mixture. While the sauce is reducing, sauté the bacon until crisp and drain on paper towels.

When the sauce has reduced to around ¾ cup, beat in the 3 remaining tablespoons of butter, one by one. Return the chicken livers to the sauce, warm through, and arrange bacon pieces on top.

SERVES TWO.

ROAST BREAST OF VEAL WITH LEMON-SAUSAGE STUFFING

A cold winter's night is the perfect time to serve this breast of veal with its flavorful stuffing of sweet Italian sausage, spinach, and lemon. It's a good idea to give your butcher advance notice when you want your meat so that he can get you a thick, succulent breast. We like to leave the bones in because they impart a wonderful flavor. The stuffed veal and bones make a handsome presentation at table, and the bones are fun to nibble. Ask the butcher to cut a pocket for stuffing and to crack the bones on the underside to facilitate slicing. The veal and its stuffing is so tender and moist that it can go without any sauce at all. But for those who desire it we include a thin, non-thickened lemon wine sauce that will not overpower the delicacy of the meat.

The breast of veal may be garnished with sticks of tender salsify sautéed in a little butter, pepped up with freshly ground pepper and salt. Follow with a zesty salad of arugola leaves dressed with a little light olive oil and lemon juice.

Start the meal with a well-chilled sparkling white wine from France or California, served with thin crisp bread coated with melted butter, sprinkled with freshly grated Parmesan cheese, and baked in a moderate (350° F.) oven for a few minutes until lightly browned. For dessert, whole peaches poached in red wine, served chilled.

WINE SUGGESTIONS: You can continue with the sparkling white wine, throughout the meal. Or uncork a light, fruity white varietal—a French Mâcon Blanc or a California Fumé Blanc.

One 7-pound breast of veal with bones in, and with pocket cut for stuffing	1½ cups lemon pulp, chopped
	½ pound fresh spinach leaves
	Salt and freshly ground pepper
1 pound sweet Italian sausage	1 teaspoon finely minced, fresh coriander, or
5 tablespoons butter	½ teaspoon dried
1 cup onion, finely minced	

3 tablespoons Italian parsley,
   finely minced
4 tablespoons Romano
   cheese, freshly grated

1 cup dry white wine or
   vermouth

Preheat oven to 350° F.

To prepare the stuffing, remove the sausage casing and sauté the sausage meat in a heavy skillet over medium heat, breaking up the pieces with a spoon as they cook so they lose their fat and become lightly browned. After about 20 minutes, remove the sausage meat to a chopping board, draining off as much fat as possible, and chop finely. If you would like an especially fine texture for the stuffing, put the meat into the container of a blender or food processor and process until fine. Turn mixture into a 2-quart bowl.

Wash and dry the skillet. Melt 3 tablespoons of the butter, add the chopped onions, and cook over medium heat for 5 to 6 minutes, stirring so they do not burn. Add the chopped lemon pulp and simmer over medium heat for about 12 minutes, or until the mixture becomes thick and glazed. Take off heat and add to the sausage mixture in the bowl.

Bring a 2-quart pot of water to a boil. Add washed, stemmed, and deveined spinach leaves and blanch the leaves for 3 minutes. Drain. Press out as much water as you can with the back of a wooden spoon. Chop finely or purée in a blender or food processor. Add the spinach purée to the sausage meat and onion-lemon mixture. Season with salt and pepper, add the minced fresh coriander (or the dried version if you cannot find the fresh in your market), the minced parsley, and the grated Romano cheese. Mix until well blended.

Stuff the veal pocket, being careful not to pack it too tightly. Secure the opening with skewers and place the breast, skin side up, in a large roasting pan. Dot with the remaining butter and pour white wine over the top. Make a loose tent with aluminum foil over the veal and roast in the preheated oven for 2½ hours. After 2 hours, remove the foil and roast until the top is golden. If the veal seems dry at this point, baste with additional melted butter combined with a little white wine.

Remove the veal to a heated platter. To facilitate carving, turn the veal bone side up and follow the butcher's crack marks.

SERVES FOUR TO SIX.

LEMON WINE SAUCE

Remove the veal to a heated platter and keep warm. Scrape the bottom of the roasting pan, deglaze with 1 cup of dry white wine, and pour the mixture into a saucepan. Add ½ cup veal stock (see page 196), 1 tablespoon glace de viande (see page 195), salt and freshly ground pepper, 2 tablespoons lemon juice, and ½ teaspoon sugar. Bring to a boil, lower heat, and simmer for 5 to 6 minutes. Pour into a heated sauceboat and pass separately.

VEAL ROULADE

Rolled roasts make handsome entrées and are especially interesting when stuffed with a combination of savory ingredients. In this case, the filling is a rich and hearty mixture of tomatoes, lemons, hot Italian sausage, and sautéed mushrooms.

It is not necessary, but it is easier to handle if you make the stuffing ahead of time and place it in the refrigerator to congeal.

Serve the veal roulade with a hearts of palm and endive salad. This looks pretty when the hearts of palm are arranged horizontally in an oval dish and the endive, sliced lengthwise, is

placed vertically over the hearts of palm. Carrot soup (see page
11) would make a nice first course. For dessert, puréed raspberries with fresh peach halves, garnished with slivered, toasted
almonds.

WINE SUGGESTION: A fruity red wine, such as a California
Gamay Beaujolais or Italian Bardolino.

1½ pounds veal sliced from the top round	½ teaspoon salt
2½ cups fresh tomatoes, peeled, seeded, and chopped	½ teaspoon sugar
	2 tablespoons butter
	½ pound fresh mushrooms, sliced
or	1½ pounds hot Italian sausage
2 28-ounce cans of peeled tomatoes, drained well	2 tablespoons olive oil
1 lemon, coarsely chopped, including peel	½ cup white wine

Ask your butcher to cut the veal into one large, rectangular
piece. Either you or he can then pound it with a mallet between
2 sheets of waxed paper to get the maximum width and length.

Preheat oven to 350° F.

Put tomatoes, chopped lemon, salt, and sugar in a saucepan
and simmer for a half hour.

In the meantime, melt the 2 tablespoons of butter in a skillet
and sauté the mushroom slices briefly over high heat. Remove
them from the skillet and set aside.

Squeeze the sausage out of the casing and crumble.

After the tomatoes have simmered for 30 minutes, add the
sautéed mushrooms and sausage and continue cooking for another
15 minutes. This can be done a day ahead.

When ready to roast, place filling down the center of the veal slice. Fold the short ends in, then pull the long sides over the filling, overlapping them slightly. Tie the long roll with string. If you have a bit too much stuffing, set it aside for the moment.

Brown the roulade in the 2 tablespoons of olive oil. Add the ½ cup of wine and place any leftover filling around the roast. Bake in the preheated oven for 45 minutes, basting several times.

SERVES FOUR.

VEAL PALLOTTA

Cheese, lemon-cream-plumped mushrooms, and flat omelets line a long, thin slice of veal which is then rolled, browned, and roasted to succulent tenderness. It is good either hot or cold. This could follow a first course of pasta tossed with butter and parsley. Accompany the pallotta with a crisp salad of sliced endive, radishes, fresh bean sprouts, and minced shallots, all tossed in a vinaigrette. For dessert, Linzertorte, rich with ground nuts and raspberries.

WINE SUGGESTION: A dry, fruity white wine, such as an Alsatian Riesling or California Johannesburg Riesling.

One 2-pound slice from leg of veal	4 tablespoons lemon juice
6 tablespoons butter	1½ teaspoons salt
4 eggs	1 large clove garlic, minced
4 tablespoons water	1 cup Italian Fontina cheese, grated
½ pound mushrooms	2 tablespoons olive oil
½ cup heavy cream	⅓ cup dry white wine

Preheat oven to 325° F.

First, the veal slice should be flattened to make a large rectangle. Next, make 2 flat omelets. To do this, melt 1½ tablespoons of the butter in an 8-inch omelet pan. Beat 2 eggs with 2 tablespoons of water until well mixed and, when butter is foaming, pour the egg mixture into pan. Reduce heat and cook, pulling edges back with a fork as they solidify and tilting the pan so the uncooked center replaces the cooked area. When the omelet is cooked but the center is slightly moist, slide it onto the upper half of the veal slice. Repeat procedure with the 2 remaining eggs, another 1½ tablespoons of butter, and the remaining water, again sliding the unfolded omelet onto the lower half of the veal.

Chop mushrooms finely and toss them in the skillet with 2 tablespoons melted butter until the butter is absorbed. Add cream, lemon juice, and salt, and cook at a low boil until mushrooms have absorbed most of the liquid, about 30 minutes. The mixture will have a brown, creamy look.

Spread mushrooms over the omelets and distribute minced garlic and grated Fontina cheese over the entire surface. Place the veal slice so that the long side faces you. Turn the 2 short ends in about 1 inch and then carefully roll up the veal from the long side, jellyroll fashion. This will give you a long roll enclosed at each end. Tie with string at intervals of 2 inches along the length of the roll, then tie once the long way, parcel fashion.

Melt the remaining tablespoon of butter and 2 tablespoons of oil in a large pan and brown the rolled veal lightly on all sides. Remove veal and deglaze the pan with the wine, scraping up any browned particles. Return veal to the pan and place it in the preheated oven. Roast for 45 minutes, basting frequently—at least 3 times—to ensure moistness and a nicely browned exterior. Remove veal roll to a heated platter and let it rest for a few minutes. Before slicing, remove strings.

Note: If your rectangle of veal is particularly narrow, it may be easier for you to roll it from the short side.

SERVES FOUR.

ROAST SHOULDER OF VEAL

A trio of flavors—fresh rosemary, lemon, and garlic—joins with golden Maderia and rich veal juices to form a redolently rich natural sauce as this veal roasts. When cooked this way the veal shoulder is succulently tender and wonderfully flavored. Serve the sliced veal on a heated platter and pass the sauce in a heated sauceboat. Or, if you prefer, spoon the sauce right over the veal slices on the platter. Puréed artichoke hearts and buttered *tubetti* —tiny pasta tubes—flecked with finely chopped Italian parsley make felicitous partners. To start this robust meal, offer a bowl of julienne strips of raw carrots and sliced raw celery tossed with a little light oil, lemon juice, and a dash of Dijon mustard. For dessert, fresh orange segments topped with toasted coconut and just a dash or two of dark Jamaican rum.

WINE SUGGESTION: A chilled, dry white wine with a bit of fruitiness, such as a German Kabinett Riesling or California Johannesburg Riesling.

One 4-pound boned shoulder of veal, rolled and tied	2 lemons, each cut into eighths
Salt and freshly ground pepper to taste	4 large cloves garlic, peeled and cut into halves

8 sprigs of fresh rosemary,
  each about 2 inches
  long, or 2 tablespoons
  dried

1 cup dry Madeira (Sercial
  or Rainwater) com-
  bined with ½ cup veal
  stock (see page 196)

Preheat oven to 350° F.

Season the veal with salt and pepper and place in a large roasting pan. Crown the top with the lemon wedges, garlic halves, and the fresh rosemary sprigs. It's the fresh rosemary that helps to make this so marvelous. However, if you don't have a pretty, pinelike rosemary plant growing on your kitchen window, use dried rosemary. Pour half the Madeira-veal-stock mixture over the meat. Roast, uncovered, 2 hours, basting with the remaining Madeira-stock mixture, adding a bit more Madeira if the meat looks dry. The lemon-rosemary-garlic crown will turn golden and brown. Don't be concerned if some of the crown falls to the bottom of the pan during roasting. The flavor will still be there. If you're serving the meat sliced on a platter, add some of the crown at either end as garniture. If you're slicing at table, add a bit of crown to each plate as you serve.

SERVES SIX.

LEMON BREADED VEAL CHOPS

The breading is light and flavorful, the chops tender and white, the result, a simple and satisfying meal that can be put together with very little time and effort. Thin noodles tossed with butter, a tablespoon of caraway seeds, and freshly ground pepper make a perfect companion for the chops. A crisp fresh chicory salad dressed with a little yogurt thinned with lemon juice and pepped up with chopped fresh mint adds texture and refreshing taste. For dessert, a basket of fresh apples, pears, and grapes, served with two cheeses—a creamy French triple crème, and a mild Italian Fontina—and a selection of biscuits.

WINE SUGGESTION: A moderately robust red wine, such as Bordeaux Supérieur or Italian Spanna.

1 egg, beaten until light	4 large loin veal chops, cut
1¼ cups very fine, dry bread	about ½-inch thick
crumbs	Salt and freshly ground
2 tablespoons parsley, very	pepper to taste
finely minced	4 tablespoons olive oil
Grated rind of 2 lemons	

Beat the egg in a shallow soup bowl or dish until light and frothy.

In another bowl combine bread crumbs, parsley, lemon rind, and mix thoroughly. Wipe chops with paper towels, and sprinkle with salt and freshly ground pepper on both sides. Dip chops into beaten egg, then coat on both sides with the bread-crumb mixture.

Heat the oil in a heavy skillet that will hold the chops without crowding. Brown over medium-high heat on one side. Lower heat and continue to cook 15 minutes, then turn heat up again and brown chops on the other side. Lower heat to simmer and continue to cook another 15 minutes, or until tender when pierced with the tines of a fork. Remove to a heated platter or plates and serve at once.

SERVES FOUR.

How to Make Perfect Bread Crumbs

We find that a French bread, made without preservatives, additives, or shortening makes perfect bread crumbs. The crumbs are delicate, and the thin crisp crust gives color and texture.

Buy the bread a day ahead. Let it stand without any wrapping at all, or with only a light covering, so that the air circulates around the bread and dries it out for at least 24 hours.

Cut the dry bread into 1-inch cubes and process in the container of a blender or food processor until fine and powdery.

Store the crumbs in a jar with a tight-fitting lid. They will keep for several weeks in the refrigerator.

BLANQUETTE DE VEAU
(Veal Stew)

The delicate cream sauce that bathes the tender chunks of veal in this dish makes it far more elegant than its designation as a stew would have you think.

In our version, the lemon juice used in the long, slow cooking of the veal makes the resulting stock a particularly piquant base for the cream and egg yolks used to finish the sauce.

Serve it with plain, steamed rice and zucchini that has been sautéed, then tossed with olive oil, vinegar, chopped garlic, anchovies, and parsley. For dessert, individual pecan tarts.

WINE SUGGESTION: An elegant, dry white wine, such as a Meursault from Burgundy or a California Chardonnay.

3 pounds shoulder of veal, cut into chunks	1 clove garlic, sliced
1 pound veal bones	1 teaspoon salt
1 medium-sized onion, studded with cloves	4 cups water
	1 cup lemon juice
3 small carrots, ends trimmed but skin left on	2 egg yolks
	1 cup heavy cream

Place the meat and bones in a large stockpot, and add onion, carrots, garlic, salt, water, and lemon juice. Bring this to a boil and skim. Reduce heat to a brisk simmer, cover, and cook for 2 hours. Check occasionally to see if further skimming is necessary. The veal should be quite tender at the end of 2 hours.

Remove meat with a slotted spoon, set aside, and discard the veal bones.

Pour the stock into a 2-quart saucepan and, over high heat, reduce to 1 cup. Put the saucepan with reduced stock into the refrigerator until any fat has solidified and can be lifted easily off the stock.

Rewarm the "cleaned" stock over medium heat. While it is warming, beat the egg yolks and heavy cream together. Add a little of the warmed stock to the egg and cream mixture, whisking well. Continue to add small amounts of the stock to the cream mixture, whisking after each addition, until the cream itself is warm. At this point, pour the cream mixture back into the stock and cook, stirring constantly, until the sauce is slightly thickened. Then add the veal to the sauce and continue cooking over low heat until the meat is warmed through. The sauce should be thick enough to coat the meat nicely, but runny enough so that when it's placed on the serving plate beside the rice there's enough to sauce the rice as well.

SERVES FOUR.

COUNTRY-STYLE LEMON VEAL LOAF

This recipe, adapted from one given us by chef Seppi Renggli, of The Four Seasons in New York, is a peasanty version of a pâté. It can be served either hot or cold, but it is best at room temperature with a bowl of cornichon pickles, chutney, and a sweet mustard.

The sturdy loaf would be nice for a weekend in the country or as the main dish at a Sunday night buffet in the city. Accompany it with a platter of steamed asparagus drenched in lemon butter and potatoes Anna. For dessert, a coffee mousse.

WINE SUGGESTION: A sturdy, dry, country red wine, such as a French Corbières, a New York State Baco Noir, or a California Ruby Cabernet.

3 pounds ground veal	1 cup fresh tomatoes,
½ pound ground pork fat	chopped
⅔ cup onions, chopped	2 teaspoons salt
½ cup Italian parsley, chopped	Freshly ground pepper
1 clove garlic, minced	6 slices bacon
1 teaspoon lemon peel, grated	2 lemons, peeled and thinly
3 eggs, lightly beaten	sliced
	Melted butter

Preheat oven to 350° F.

Combine the veal, pork fat, onion, parsley, garlic, lemon peel, eggs, tomatoes, and seasonings. These should be well mixed. Really the best way to do it is to integrate the ingredients thoroughly with your hands. Form the mixture into a loaf and place in a shallow baking dish that has been lined with bacon. Cover the loaf with thin slices of lemon. Bake in the preheated oven for 1 hour. Remove the lemon slices, baste with melted butter, and return to oven for 15 minutes to brown lightly.

SERVES SIX.

A LAMB AND GOLDEN LEMON AILLADE

"Too heavenly" is the way Richard Olney, painter, cook, and author, describes the way he prepares lamb shanks—braised and sauced with the aromatic herbs of Provence, where he lives. Cognac, white wine, and lemon also flavor the lamb shanks, which are garnished with an incredible amount of garlic, but simmered until the garlic's aggressive disposition has turned to a sweet and delicately nutty flavor.

"Readers suspicious of such a generous quantity of garlic will be astonished at the gentle sweetness of its character," Olney explains. He also talks of fresh hyssop leaves, which may be replaced by parsley. "Hyssop is a labiate herb, cousin to thyme, rosemary, marjoram and the mints, one of the sacred herbs of the ancients, nearly forgotten today, but rustic and easily grown. The seeds should be started in seed boxes and the seedlings transplanted to pots, window boxes or out-of-doors borders; perennial in the Mediterranean climate, the tiny, intense blue flowers also are a wonderful salad decor. The leaves have an exhilarating, 'wild' perfume and a delicately bitter, refreshing flavor that falls into perfect harmony with the lamb-garlic-lemon alliance."

Olney suggests serving the lamb shanks directly from the casserole, accompanied by steamed rice or an unflavored pilaf. We like to start this pungent meal with the thinnest possible slices of Scotch salmon drizzled with a little lemon juice and a hail of cracked black pepper. For dessert, in deference to Olney, who is not a dessert fancier, a plate of crisp thin *gaufrettes* and Château d'Yquem.

WINE SUGGESTION: With the lamb, Olney suggests a Bandol from Provence, a mouth-filling wine that goes well with robust dishes.

THE LAMB

- 3 tablespoons olive oil
- 4 lamb shanks, or 2½ pounds of shoulder, cut across the bone into 4 pieces
- 1 large onion, coarsely chopped
- Salt, a pinch of cayenne, a bit of freshly ground allspice, and a small bay leaf
- 1 teaspoon dried herbs (thyme, oregano, marjoram)
- 2 teaspoons sugar
- 3 tablespoons flour
- ¼ cup Cognac
- 1 cup dry white wine
- ⅔ cup canned Italian plum tomatoes
- About 1½ cups boiling water (to almost cover meat)

THE GARNISH

| 20 or 30 crisp, fresh (no green sprouts), peeled garlic cloves, parboiled at a simmer for 15 minutes and drained | Freshly ground pepper to taste |
| 1 small lemon, pared free of white pith, cut into 6 slices | 1 tablespoon grated lemon rind mixed with 1 tablespoon fresh hyssop leaves, finely chopped (substitute ½ cup chopped fresh parsley, if necessary) |

Heat the oil and color pieces of lamb over medium heat in a heavy pot large enough to hold them comfortably without crowding. After approximately 15 minutes, add onions and seasonings, and stir regularly. As the onions begin to take on a caramel color, sprinkle them with sugar. Continue stirring and turning the meat. A couple of minutes later, sprinkle with flour; stir and turn pieces of meat 2 or 3 times until the flour is lightly browned.

Turn up heat. Add the Cognac and stir until the pan is dry; add the wine and continue to stir and scrape free any caramelized flour or meat juices adhering to pan. When the meat pieces are thoroughly coated with a thick sauce, add tomatoes and enough water nearly to cover. Stir, bring to a boil, and adjust heat (using an asbestos pad, if necessary) so that with the pot covered, a bare simmer is maintained. Cook gently for 1½ hours, turning meat over in the sauce once or twice, then degrease. (Skim off fat that arises to the top and discard.)

Remove pieces of meat to a plate. Pass the contents of the pan through a fine sieve into a small saucepan. Return meat to the pan and scatter over the parboiled garlic and the lemon slices over the meat. Keep the contents warm and covered while cleansing the sauce.

To cleanse, bring the sauce to a boil and adjust heat so that, with saucepan drawn somewhat to the side of the flame, one half of the surface is maintained at a light boil, the other half remaining still. Leave to reduce gently and, as a skin forms on the silent surface, carefully pull it off to the side with a spoon, lift it out, and discard it. Repeat several times over a period of about 20 minutes until a skin no longer forms.

Pour sauce over the meat and its garnish and simmer, covered, for another 20 minutes, shaking pan gently from time to time. Add freshly ground pepper to taste. Sprinkle the surface with the mixture of grated lemon rind and hyssop (or parsley) and serve directly from the casserole, accompanied by steamed rice or an unflavored pilaf.

SERVES FOUR.

LAMB STEW SANS PAREIL

A fabulous cold-weather dish, this lamb stew is especially delectable because it uses the leg of lamb. Tender chunks of meat are simmered in an aromatic broth that is thickened with lemon pulp and tomatoes. Tarragon, garlic, and Cognac give it a flavor that's *sans pareil*. Serve the stew with steamed wheat pilaf (recipe follows) to catch all the wonderful sauce. Tiny Belgian carrots sautéed in butter with a bit of chopped parsley or dill make a colorful garniture. Start the meal with apéritifs and a bowl of raw white mushrooms, with a curry-spiked mayonnaise as a dipping sauce. For dessert, a rich, silken cheesecake and lots of hot espresso.

WINE SUGGESTION: A full-bodied and mature red Bordeaux, such as a Saint-Emilion or a California Cabernet Sauvignon.

4 pounds lamb, cut from the leg into 2-inch pieces, with all fat and gristle removed

4 tablespoons olive oil, or more, as needed

½ cup Cognac

1½ cups onion, finely minced

1 clove garlic, finely minced

Salt and freshly ground pepper to taste

1 teaspoon fresh tarragon, finely minced, or ½ teaspoon dried

1½ cups dry white wine

1½ cups fresh ripe tomatoes, peeled, seeded, and chopped

2 cups beef stock or bouillon (see page 194)

4 sprigs parsley, tied with thread

2 lemons, peel on, thinly sliced, then quartered

3 tablespoons curly parsley, finely chopped— heads only

In a heavy 5-quart Dutch oven brown lamb pieces in olive oil over brisk heat until colored on all sides. Add Cognac and again cook over brisk heat for 3 minutes. Add onions, garlic, seasonings, white wine, tomatoes, and stock or bouillon. Lamb should be just covered with liquid. If it isn't, add additional bouillon to cover. Tuck in parsley and season with salt and pepper. Bring liquid to a boil, stirring a bit. Lower heat to simmer, cover pot, and simmer for 1½ to 2 hours. Discard parsley after the first hour. Lift the lid now and then and skim off the grease that rises to the top.

When meat is tender, remove with a slotted spoon and keep warm. Transfer sauce to a small saucepan and cook over medium heat until reduced about one-third. This should take about 30 minutes. From time to time, skim off the skin that forms on the top of the sauce.

Return meat to Dutch oven and lay quartered lemon slices on top. Pour sauce over and simmer, gently, over low heat for 15 to 20 minutes. Sprinkle with chopped parsley and serve.

SERVES EIGHT.

BULGHUR OR WHEAT PILAF

3 tablespoons butter
2 cups bulghur or wheat pilaf
¼ cup onion, grated
3½ cups rich beef stock
   (see page 194)

½ cup lemon juice
Salt and freshly ground
   pepper to taste

Melt the butter in a saucepan, add the wheat pilaf, and cook over medium heat, stirring, for several minutes, until the grains are golden and glistening. Add the grated onion and cook another 2 minutes, stirring. Add the stock and the lemon juice, turn up heat, and cook at a brisk pace until the liquid is absorbed by the grains, about 10 minutes. You will have to watch the pot to see that the bottom does not burn. As soon as the liquid is absorbed, set the pot on an asbestos pad, season the pilaf with salt and pepper, cover, and keep warm over low heat. If you use a heavy saucepan, such as the enameled cast iron type, the bulghur may be kept warm this way for an hour, or so.

SERVES EIGHT.

LEMON-LARDED LEG OF LAMB

Leg of lamb is rendered succulent by inserting bits of lemon pulp, garlic, and rosemary into the flesh, which self-bastes and flavors the lamb as it is roasting. We like the lamb served pink, in the French manner. It has a totally different flavor and texture from well-done lamb, but, of course, this is purely a matter of taste. The sliced meat may be garnished with flageolets, small, dried, green kidney beans, and braised endive. Smoked trout served with a mustard-cream sauce is a first course that complements the lamb. For dessert, Chaource cheese from the Champagne area in France with green grapes.

WINE SUGGESTION: A dry, red wine with medium body and some elegance, such as a Saint-Emilion from Bordeaux or a vintage Cabernet Sauvignon from California.

> One 7- to 8-pound leg of lamb
> 2 lemons, peeled, seeded, and the pulp chopped
> 2 to 3 large cloves garlic, finely diced
> 3 tablespoons fresh rosemary, finely chopped

Preheat oven to 350° F.

Be sure the fell (the thin membrane covering the leg) has been removed by the butcher, or peel it off yourself. Trim away as much fat as possible. Using the point of a sharp knife, make slits about ¼-inch deep over the surface of the lamb at intervals of approximately 1 inch. Still using the tip of the knife, push some of the lemon pulp into some of the slits; alternate by inserting diced garlic into some of the other slits. You needn't be too precise about the amounts of lemon pulp and garlic, as the flavors will meld once the roast is in the oven. Finally, dust the top of the lamb with the chopped rosemary. Roast the lamb in the preheated oven: 15 minutes per pound for rare; 20 minutes for medium rare; 25 minutes for well done.

SERVES EIGHT.

DAUBE OF BEEF

Several hours of simmering bring the beef to the point where it may be cut with a fork. Aromatic herbs, chopped shallots, lemons, and Cognac integrate into an unusual and natural sauce. It's particularly nice to cook this on a bleak, icy winter day.

Since the beef and its self-made sauce make a robust dish, only a light beginning is needed—a cup of good beef or chicken broth enlivened with a dash of sherry and garnished, Japanese style, with a few rounds of green scallions. Steamed bulghur wheat and spinach that is tossed with melted butter and a grating of nutmeg accompany the beef. For dessert, a compote of apples, prunes, golden raisins, and fresh orange segments, served warm in individual crockery dishes. Pass a bottle of Cointreau for guests to spoon over the fruit as they like and brew lots of espresso.

WINE SUGGESTION: A full-bodied, somewhat assertive red wine, such as Chianti Classico, Côtes du Rhone, or California Petite Sirah.

3½ pounds brisket of beef
1 cup Cognac
3 tablespoons shallots, finely minced
1 clove garlic, peeled and finely minced
½ cup dry red wine
1 cup lemon, finely chopped with peel on
1 bouquet garni: one 3-inch piece of celery with leaves, 6 sprigs parsley, and ¼ teaspoon dried sage tied in a cheesecloth bag
Salt and freshly ground pepper to taste
¼ teaspoon cracked allspice
⅛ teaspoon ground ginger

Sear meat on all sides. Add Cognac and step well aside, as it will smoke. When smoking subsides, add all remaining ingredients, including the bouquet garni. Cover tightly and simmer 2½ to 3 hours, turning meat once during the cooking process. Slice meat to desired thickness and return it to the pot to simmer for another 20 minutes. If a smoother sauce is preferred, take meat out and put sauce through a food mill or purée it in a food processor.

SERVES FOUR.

GOLDEN LEMON LONDON BROIL

There are many cuts of beef that can be, and are, prepared as London broil—the thin, sinewy flank, the shoulder, chuck, or top or bottom round, to name some. All are well suited for marinating and grilling.

We like top sirloin for its tender texture and flavor. The meat is first marinated in lemon juice, mustard, herbs, and garlic—a combination that tenderizes and imparts a zingy flavor—then grilled to desired doneness. The exterior is crusty, the inside, succulent. Serve the meat sliced on the thin side, with a garniture of oven-roasted potato halves and a crisp, fresh cabbage slaw dressed with homemade mayonnaise combined with sour cream and pepped up with caraway seeds. Start the meal with a mound of peasanty chicken-liver pâté served with crisp red radishes or slices of zesty black radishes, if you can find them in the market. For dessert, homemade apple pie and wedges of sharp cheddar cheese.

WINE SUGGESTION: A hearty, full-bodied country wine, such as a French Corbières or Cahors, a California Zinfandel, or New York State Chancellor.

2½ pounds top sirloin	chervil, oregano,
½ cup lemon juice	marjoram, and tarragon
½ cup dry red wine	or 1 teaspoon dried
3 teaspoons Dijon mustard	herbs of your choice
1 large clove garlic, finely	¼ cup light olive oil
minced	Salt and freshly ground
3 teaspoons mixed fresh	pepper
herbs, finely minced:	

Place the meat in a bowl. Beat together the remaining ingredients and pour over the meat. Cover the bowl and refrigerate 8 to 24 hours, turning the meat several times. When ready to broil, remove the meat from the marinade and sprinkle with salt. Sear it on a hot grill on both sides, then broil, basting with the marinade: 10 minutes to the pound for rare; 15 minutes for medium rare; 20 minutes for well done. Slice thinly on the diagonal.

SERVES SIX TO EIGHT.

Note: This is effectively done on an outdoor grill, the sliced meat placed between toasted, buttered rolls after grilling.

SWEET-AND-SOUR TONGUE

There is an added plus to the great flavor of this savory sauced, tender tongue. The entire dish can be made a day or two ahead, and then needs only a few minutes of gentle simmering before bringing it to table. Either smoked or pickled tongue is appropriate; it's really a matter of individual taste. The smoked, of course, has a slightly smoke-cured flavor; the pickled, a sharper, more seasoned taste. But it's the sauce in which the slices of tongue are finally simmered, with its opposite elements of yin and yang —sweet and sour—that gives this dish its standout flavor.

Serve the tongue with steamed potatoes and new green cabbage braised in butter and enlivened with caraway seeds. For dessert, scoops of peach, vanilla, and chocolate ice cream arranged in a chilled glass bowl and topped with lightly toasted coconut shreds.

WINE SUGGESTION: The piquantly sauced tongue needs an assertive red wine, such as a Côtes du Rhone or California Petite Sirah.

THE MEAT
> One 4-pound smoked or pickled beef tongue
> Water to cover

THE SWEET-AND-SOUR SAUCE

4 tablespoons butter	¼ cup red wine vinegar
¾ cup onions, thinly sliced	4 teaspoons sugar
2 teaspoons flour	Freshly ground pepper
¼ cup lemon juice	to taste
1½ cups beef stock (see	½ cup golden raisins
page 194)	

Wash the tongue under cold running water, place in a 6-quart
Dutch oven, and cover with cold water. Bring to a boil, lower
flame, cover, and simmer the tongue for 3½ to 4 hours, or until
the meat, at the thickest part, is tender when pierced with the
tines of a fork. Check the tongue from time to time while it is
cooking, and add additional water if it is not completely covered.
When done, carefully remove the tongue and allow it to cool
enough to handle. Then cut off the fat and bones from the thick
end and, using a sharp paring knife, peel off the thick skin. If the
tongue has been cooked until tender, the skin will peel readily. If
you are planning to save the tongue to be used in the next day or
two, wrap it securely in plastic and store it in the refrigerator.
When ready to use, cut the tongue into slices as thin or thick as
desired, ready for saucing.

To prepare the sauce, melt the butter in a heavy saucepan,
add the onions, and cook over a very low flame until they are
golden, about 5 to 8 minutes. Add the 2 teaspoons of flour, stirring with a wooden spoon until it is absorbed. Add the lemon
juice, then the stock, stirring until smooth. Cover and simmer over
very low heat while you prepare the sweet and sour elements. Heat
the red wine vinegar in a small saucepan. Add the sugar, and
cook, stirring, over brisk heat for 5 to 6 minutes, or until the mixture is lightly syrupy. Spoon the mixture into the master sauce and
stir to combine flavors. Add freshly ground pepper to taste. (Salt is

not necessary, as the tongue itself contains salt.) If the sauce is not quite tart enough, add additional lemon juice. Add the golden raisins and simmer for a few minutes longer.

If you are using the sauce over just-cooked tongue, place the tongue slices on a heated platter and spoon the sauce on top. If you are using tongue prepared ahead and refrigerated, place the slices in a skillet large enough to hold the tongue and the sauce. Pour the sauce from the saucepan over the slices in the skillet and heat gently for 5 to 10 minutes.

SERVES EIGHT.

STUFFED CABBAGE ROLLS

There are as many variants of stuffed cabbage rolls as there are leaves in a head of cabbage. This one is tart with an undertone of sweetness. The savory rolls are cooked with fresh ripe tomatoes, apples, onions, and lemon, which flavor and thicken the sauce naturally. Plan on about 40 minutes to assemble the cabbage and meat rolls, but once in the covered pot, there's nothing more to do but check once in a while to see that they're covered with liquid. If not, add a little water. The rolls make a hearty entrée, with the addition of plain boiled rice and a salad of sweet red peppers, roasted over a flame, peeled, seeded and dressed with a little oil, vinegar, and perhaps a touch of garlic. For dessert, chocolate fudge squares dusted with a little confectioners' sugar.

WINE SUGGESTION: A sturdy red wine of little pretension is the best companion for the lively flavors of the cabbage rolls, such as a California mountain red, a French country red or an Italian non-Classico Chianti.

1 leafy green cabbage	Salt and freshly ground
3 cups onions, thinly sliced	pepper
3 cups apples, peeled, cored, and thinly sliced	2 pounds finely ground chuck
2 cups red-ripe tomatoes, peeled, seeded, and chopped	1 tablespoon onion, grated
	½ cup tomato juice
½ cup lemon juice	1 tablespoon sugar

It's easier to separate the cabbage leaves if the cabbage is parboiled, so bring a large pot of water to a boil, add the washed cabbage head, and simmer for 10 minutes. Drain and cool the cabbage. Line the bottom of a heavy 5-quart casserole with the sliced onions, apples, and chopped tomatoes. Add ¼ cup of the lemon juice, a little salt and freshly ground pepper.

In a large bowl mix the meat with the grated onion and the tomato juice.

Core the cooled cabbage with a sharp knife and carefully remove the leaves. You should have about 12 leaves. Choose the large, green leaves as they are the most tender. Cut out the hard vein at the end of each leaf. Place about 2 tablespoons of the meat mixture in the center of each leaf, making certain there's enough border of cabbage all around to fold. Fold the cabbage leaves over the meat, tucking in the ends to make a neat bundle. Place the rolls on top of the onion-apple mixture.

Add the sugar and the remaining lemon juice. Cover the pot and simmer gently for 2½ to 3 hours. Taste to correct seasonings. You may like a bit more lemon or a touch more sugar.

SERVES FOUR.

FRICASSEE DE PORC AUX CITRONS
(Fricassée of Pork with Lemons)

Michel Guérard, chef and owner of the three-Michelin-star restaurant, Les Prés d'Eugénie, in the Landes, just east of the Basque country in France, gave us this recipe for fricassée of pork with lemon. It is an unusually delicate handling of pork, and the sauce—which contains no flour—is suave and elegant. Garnish the dish with tiny potato balls dusted with minced parsley and serve a basket of French bread. The meal could start with eggplant caviar—eggplant baked, then puréed or finely chopped, and blended with lemon juice, olive oil, salt, pepper, and a zip of grated onion. Chill well and serve on a lettuce leaf or with crackers. For dessert, poached peaches sauced with a purée of blackberries.

WINE SUGGESTION: A light, fruity young Beaujolais or California Gamay Beaujolais.

2 pounds boneless loin of
    pork, cut into 1½-inch
    cubes
¼ cup onion, thinly sliced
¼ cup lemon juice
1½ tablespoons orange juice
½ cup dry white wine
1 cup chicken stock (see
    page 198)
Salt and freshly ground
    pepper to taste

¼ cup wine vinegar
5 teaspoons sugar
6 tablespoons crème fraîche
    (see page 200)
2 lemons, peeled and cut
    into quarters
Zests of 1 lemon and an
    orange quarter cut into
    fine julienne strips

Marinate the pieces of pork overnight with the onions, lemon and orange juices, and the white wine. The next morning transfer the pork and the marinade to a heavy casserole. Add the chicken stock and season with salt and pepper to taste. Cook, covered, over medium heat for 1 hour. Using a slotted spoon, lift out the pieces of pork, set aside, and keep warm.

Reduce the cooking liquid in the casserole by one-third. While it is reducing, combine the vinegar and the sugar in a small saucepan, bring to a boil, and cook until the mixture becomes light brown and syrupy. (*Authors' note:* This will take only about 5 minutes and must be watched carefully so that the sugar doesn't burn.) Stir in the crème fraîche until well blended. Add the contents of the small saucepan to the cooking liquid in the casserole, stirring to blend thoroughly, and check the seasoning. Cook another 10 minutes to reduce the sauce a bit more.

Prepare the quarters of lemon and the julienne strips of lemon and orange. (*Authors' note:* It's a good idea to boil the julienne strips a minute or two, then drain them in a strainer to rid them of any bitterness.)

Place the pieces of pork on hot plates. Cover with the sauce and sprinkle with the orange and lemon zest. Garnish with the lemon quarters and serve at once.

SERVES FOUR.

STUFFED HAM

Every day, Eli Zabar lines up freshly made delicacies on an immense butcher block table in his New York food store, E.A.T.

There are baskets of warm, buttery croissants, bowls of ratatouille, and this ham, stuffed with dried fruits, then slowly baked and basted with a concoction that turns it into a glazed marvel. Eli says, "This slow baking and basting makes the flavors of the fruit permeate the ham and the sweetness on the outside goes in."

Almost any boiled ham can be used—round, pear-shaped, or a canned Polish ham. We use a 3-pound canned Polish ham, but the amount of dried fruit and the basting mixture can easily be adjusted for a larger ham.

If you make this in summer when fresh corn on the cob is available, a big bowl of corn with lots of slightly softened sweet butter, salt, and pepper would make a delicious accompaniment, along with a cold cucumber salad. In winter, serve the ham with potatoes Boulangère—thinly sliced potatoes and onions baked in a slow oven—and eggplant mousse. For dessert, a glazed pineapple tart.

WINE SUGGESTIONS: Champagne is perfect with ham; or a fruity Beaujolais, such as a Brouilly or Moulin-à-Vent.

One 3-pound canned Polish ham	Cloves
Peel of ½ lemon, finely minced	1 tablespoon honey
⅔ cup mixed dried fruit, coarsely chopped	½ cup brown sugar
	½ cup cream sherry
	Juice of 1 lemon

When you buy the ham, ask the butcher to remove it from the tin and cut a hole about the size of a quarter through the center of the meat. If you use a larger ham, the hole should be proportionately larger. Or, you can cut a hole in the ham yourself, but you will need a long, sharp knife.

Preheat oven to 350° F.

Stuff the hole with the minced lemon peel and chopped, dried fruit—it might be a mixture of dried apricots, pears, and prunes, although any pitted, dried fruit can be used. After you have forced the dried fruit and peel into the ham, take 2 slices of dried pineapple or 2 large apricot slices and cover the holes at either end to keep the stuffing in place. Tie the ham with a string to hold the dried fruit on either end.

Stud the ham lavishly with cloves, place in a roasting pan, and put in the preheated oven, without any liquid, for 15 minutes. The ham must be quite hot to receive the basting liquid.

While the ham is warming up, combine the honey, brown sugar, sherry, and lemon juice in a small saucepan. Heat and stir until the mixture liquefies. After the ham has been in the oven for 15 minutes, start basting it with the honey-sherry mixture. Cook the ham for 45 additional minutes, basting every 15 minutes. It should bake for 1 hour in all. When done, remove ham from the oven and place it on a platter.

If you wish to serve the ham with a sauce—although it is marvelous all by itself—pour the basting liquid out of the roasting pan into a saucepan, add a few raisins, a little more sherry or water, and cook the mixture briefly over a high flame until it is the consistency you wish.

This ham is also delicious cold, thinly sliced and served with a mixture of cold, cooked vegetables vinaigrette.

SERVES FOUR TO SIX.

VARIATION

You can use the meat cut out from the center of the ham for a pleasant breakfast or brunch dish:

> 1 tablespoon butter
> 1 cup sliced boiled ham
> 2 teaspoons lemon peel, grated
> 2 eggs

Melt butter and add the ham and grated lemon peel. Sauté the ham until it is slightly browned. Carefully break 2 eggs onto the ham. Cover and cook until whites are just set.

SERVES TWO.

PORK ROAST WITH LEMON GLAZE

Rosemary, Cognac, and lemon are used to baste this loin of pork which becomes meltingly tender with a rich, brown glaze when done. Serve it with potatoes that have been thinly sliced and sautéed until tender on top and crisply brown beneath, and a platter of steamed asparagus with butter. For dessert, poached apple slices with caramel or butterscotch sauce.

WINE SUGGESTION: A full-bodied, zesty California red, such as Zinfandel, or an earthy Italian Valtelline red—Inferno or Grumello, made from grapes grown in the foothills of the Alps.

One 4-pound, boned loin of   ½ cup sugar
   pork, unrolled   ½ cup lemon juice
4 tablespoons rosemary   3 tablespoons Cognac
1 cup white wine

Preheat oven to 450° F.

The loin is left unrolled to facilitate marinating. First, slash meat with the grain at various intervals and stuff liberally with about 3 tablespoons of the rosemary. Place it in a container that will accommodate the length of the pork. Pour white wine over the meat and sprinkle the remaining rosemary over the top. Marinate for 1½ hours, turning meat a couple of times. Remove meat from marinade, pat dry, and roll into a cylindrical shape. Tie with thread.

Place meat in the preheated oven for 15 minutes, then reduce heat to 350° F. After 30 minutes, baste with fat from the roast.

Mix sugar, lemon juice, and Cognac and stir to dissolve the sugar. When the roast has cooked for 1 hour, remove from oven and pour off the fat. Spoon the lemon-Cognac mixture over the roast and return to oven. Cook for an additional 30 minutes, basting the roast with the glaze every 5 or 10 minutes. Glaze should become thick and the roast a glossy brown when done. Remove from oven and let sit for a few minutes before slicing.

SERVES FOUR TO SIX.

The roast is also good cold, sliced and served with Dijon mustard, cornichon pickles, and a small salad.

PASTA BIZANZIA
(Cold, Fresh Tomato Sauce with Pasta)

We first encountered this fresh tomato sauce at the Pisa de Torre restaurant in Milan. It is made from uncooked, chopped, fresh tomatoes, generous splashes of lemon juice, and minced garlic. The juxtaposition of the cold, fresh tomatoes on top of the hot pasta is a remarkable sensation. At Pisa de Torre, the sauce was mounded on top of the pasta, a large sprig of fresh basil placed in the center, and olive oil in a little flask was passed separately along with a pepper mill. You pour as much olive oil as you want on top of the sauce, grind on the pepper, cut up the basil leaves, and devour the pasta as gracefully as possible. It's like tasting tomatoes for the first time. At Pisa de Torre, the pasta was followed by thick slices of veal, Gattinara wine, and a great sense of satisfaction. We can suggest nothing better. Remember, the tomatoes must be superb—vine ripened and richly red. For dessert, an assortment of cookies—pecan wafers, shortbread hearts, and honey cakes.

10 tomatoes, peeled	Scant teaspoon salt
⅓ to ½ cup lemon juice	1 pound linguine, cooked
3 cloves garlic, finely minced	al dente
	4 sprigs fresh basil

Peel the tomatoes by dropping them into boiling water for a few minutes; remove and run under cold water—the skins will slip off. Core tomatoes and squeeze gently to remove excess juice. Place whole, skinned tomatoes in a bowl and chop. Add lemon juice, garlic, and salt; stir thoroughly.

Boil 1 pound linguine until *al dente*. When done, drain and mound the linguine on 4 plates. Place a generous amount of the tomato sauce on top, center it with a sprig of fresh basil, and serve at once. Pass a flask of very good olive oil and fresh pepper and have available a small bowl with more fresh basil.

SERVES FOUR.

CLAM SAUCE WITH TAGLIATELLE

A luscious tomato sauce, thick with fresh plump clams, served over hot tagliatelle—ribbons of egg noodles—makes a simple but perfect meal. The sauce has lots of garlic, clam juice, and lemon to give it character. All that's needed to complement the dish is a salad of tossed fresh greens. For dessert, a ripe Gorgonzola cheese and fresh peaches.

WINE SUGGESTION: A light Italian red wine, such as Bardolino or Valpolicella.

5 cloves garlic
¾ cup olive oil
1 cup clam juice
½ cup lemon juice
1½ cups tomato paste
1 teaspoon sugar
1 teaspoon salt

4 dozen Littleneck clams, shucked
4 tablespoons parsley, chopped
1 pound tagliatelle, cooked al dente

Sauté the garlic in olive oil briefly, being careful not to brown. Add clam and lemon juices, tomato paste, sugar, and salt. Stir and simmer for about 5 minutes, until the sauce is well mixed and hot. Add clams, cook until heated through, and stir in parsley.

Boil tagliatelle until *al dente,* drain, and place in a large bowl. Toss with a small amount of sauce—just enough to coat the pasta lightly. Divide the pasta among 4 plates and spoon remaining sauce on top of each portion at table.

SERVES FOUR.

PASTA SAUCE I

This and the following pasta sauces are for those occasions when you want to prepare a quick dinner that is special and delicious. They are most appropriate for two people and basically rely on little, leftover ingredients, such as half a zucchini, a couple of mushrooms, or a few slices of prosciutto ham. Once familiarized with these sauces, other combinations will occur to you, depending on what you have around.

Since the basic premise of these sauces is to make something tasteful in a limited amount of time, the rest of the meal can be equally simple—a salad of watercress and chopped endive in a mustard vinaigrette. For dessert, apples and a Pont l'Evèque.

WINE SUGGESTION: A lighthearted red Italian wine, such as Valpolicella or Chianti.

2 tablespoons butter
3 tablespoons scallions, chopped

2 fresh mushrooms, julienned
1 teaspoon salt

2 small tomatoes, peeled,
   seeded, and chopped
¼ cup lemon juice
½ cup chicken stock

1 cup heavy cream
½ pound linguine, cooked
   al dente

Melt butter in a skillet, add scallions, and sauté over low heat for 1 minute; then add julienned mushrooms and salt. Cook gently for a few more minutes and add chopped tomatoes. Continue cooking until tomatoes have melted into the other ingredients. Add lemon juice and chicken stock, raise heat, and cook until the liquid has been reduced to about ¼ cup. Add cream and continue cooking over moderate heat for a few minutes, until sauce has thickened.

Divide cooked, drained linguine between 2 large plates and pour sauce into the center of each mound of pasta.

The mushrooms and tomatoes can be eliminated from this recipe, although they do add definite flavor and texture. The cream, however, must always be the heavy kind used for whipping; it will not curdle when boiled and thickens naturally when heated with reduced stock.

SERVES TWO.

PASTA SAUCE II

Italian Fontina—a good cheese for melting—and sautéed bacon are the primary ingredients in this sauce. For a different but simple salad accompaniment, serve arugola tossed in a walnut oil vinaigrette. For dessert, stir chopped, glacéed marrons into slightly softened vanilla ice cream.

WINE SUGGESTION: A light, dry red wine, such as Italian Bardolino or California Barbera.

4 slices bacon	¼ cup white wine
2 tablespoons shallots or scallions, chopped	½ cup Italian Fontina cheese, grated
Juice of 1 lemon	½ pound linguine, cooked
1 tablespoon tomato paste	al dente

Sauté bacon until crisp, remove, crumble, and set aside. Add chopped shallots to the pan and cook until limp. Stir in lemon juice, tomato paste, and wine; cook briefly, about 3 to 4 minutes. Put the grated Fontina cheese into a bowl large enough to contain the linguine. Cook and drain the pasta; place it immediately in the bowl containing the cheese and toss. The cheese will melt slightly and coat the linguine. Add the shallot mixture and toss again. Scatter reserved bacon over the pasta and serve.

SERVES TWO.

PASTA SAUCE III

Fresh ricotta cheese is tossed with hot noodles and a tomato sauce is poured on top for this version of a fast pasta dish.

Since you have tomatoes as a sauce, you could omit a salad and have instead, as a first course, hot artichokes. Remove the chokes and fill with melted butter, a few bread crumbs, and chopped parsley. Or cook the artichokes ahead of time and, just before serving, remove the chokes and fill with mayonnaise. For dessert, a plate of tiny Linzertortes.

WINE SUGGESTION: A medium-bodied, dry red wine, such as New York State Baco Noir or Italian Chianti.

1 clove garlic, minced	½ teaspoon salt
1 tablespoon olive oil	¼ teaspoon sugar
One 28-ounce can of peeled	White wine, as needed
tomatoes, well drained	½ pound noodles, cooked
2 thick slices of lemon with	al dente
peel left on,	½ pound fresh ricotta
coarsely chopped	cheese

Cook garlic in olive oil briefly, being careful not to brown. Add tomatoes, lemon, salt, and sugar, and simmer for 35 to 40 minutes. If more liquid is needed during cooking time, add a little white wine.

Cook noodles *al dente*. Drain and toss with ricotta cheese in a serving bowl. Pour tomato sauce on top.

SERVES TWO.

BLACK BEAN SOUP

A good, hot black bean soup is wonderful fare on cold winter nights when the wind is whistling. This recipe is a lively combination of black beans, Burgundy wine, lemon juice, and vegetables. Thick and satisfying, it can be made into an entire meal by adding sliced Italian sausage when the soup is done. Black pumpernickel fingers toasted, buttered lavishly, and piled into a napkin-lined basket would go well with the soup, and you could also serve little bowls of chopped green pepper and onions as garnish.

For dessert, a pot de pomme—apple slices covered with a crumbly mixture of butter, sugar, and flour, baked until all is thick and glazed, then topped with sour cream and grated maple sugar and popped into the oven until the cream has set and the maple sugar starts to melt.

WINE SUGGESTION: A pale-dry Fino sherry, served chilled, would be lovely with the soup.

1 pound black beans	1 teaspoon salt
3 cloves garlic, minced	2 cups red Burgundy wine
6 small carrots, chopped	½ cup lemon juice
1 medium-sized onion, chopped	

Wash beans and soak in water overnight. Drain, rinse, and place in a kettle with water to cover. Bring to a boil, reduce heat, cover pot, and maintain a gentle boil for 1½ hours.

You may have to add water during the 1½-hour period. Check every half-hour, and if beans have absorbed most of the liquid, pour in 1 glass of water. At the end of the 1½ hours, add garlic, carrots, onions, and salt. Cook for another half-hour, or until vegetables are soft. Put the mixture through a sieve or food mill, or purée in a blender; add wine and lemon juice and simmer until heated through. If the soup is too thick, add equal parts of Burgundy and stock until soup attains the desired consistency.

SERVES FOUR AS A MAIN COURSE.

LENTIL SOUP

The meat from the pork hock or ham bone that's cooked in this hearty soup can be sliced right into it when the soup is finished.

Or the bones can be removed and thick rounds of plump, zesty knackwurst or other wurst may be added at serving time.

The soup improves with reheating. Serve lentil soup in large, deep, prewarmed soup bowls. Add a basket of crusty rye and pumpernickel breads, a crock of sweet butter, a good, robust cheese, such as Black Diamond Cheddar or Swiss Gruyère for a satisfying cold-weather lunch or Sunday supper. For dessert, winter pears poached in a thin sugar syrup and garnished with unsweetened whipped cream flecked with a bit of grated lemon zest.

WINE SUGGESTION: The aggressive flavors of the soup require a zesty, full-bodied red wine, such as a California Zinfandel or a purple-hued Petite Sirah.

2½ cups lentils, washed and drained	1 teaspoon mixed dried herbs—marjoram, thyme, and chervil
1 ham bone or smoked pork hock	Freshly ground pepper to taste
1 cup onion, finely chopped	
1½ cups carrots, finely chopped	3 quarts beef stock or beef bouillon (see page 194)
1½ cups turnips, finely chopped	1 cup dry red wine
6 sprigs Italian parsley	⅔ cup lemon juice
1 small bay leaf	1½ pounds zesty wurst, optional

Use a large stockpot or a 6-quart Dutch oven. Add the drained lentils, the ham bone or smoked pork hock, the chopped onion, carrots and turnips, parsley sprigs, bay leaf, herbs, pepper, and lemon juice. Add the stock and red wine and bring to a boil. Lower heat and simmer, uncovered, for 2½ to 3 hours. Skim surface frequently and remove the parsley sprigs after the first hour, as they turn bitter with long cooking.

When ready to serve, remove ham bone or smoked pork hocks and slice some of the meat, carefully removing gristle and fat. Turn the meat back into the soup.

Or skin and parboil the knackwurst and slice into rounds about ⅓-inch thick. Divide among 4 large, warmed soup bowls. Ladle soup over the wurst and serve at once.

The remaining soup may be kept in the refrigerator 4 or 5 days and reheated.

SERVES FOUR.

VEGETABLES

EGGPLANT BOLOGNESE

Eggplant is a wonderful vegetable that adapts itself to cheeses, sauces, and other vegetables with splendid results.

In this dish, it is layered with fresh mozzarella cheese and a tomato sauce made with prosciutto ham, cream, and lemon juice. It could accompany a glazed ham for a festive holiday meal but would be equally nice served with an egg dish—mushroom omelets, for instance, or creamy scrambled eggs with parsley. It is also good with buttered noodles.

Precede any of these with asparagus soup. For dessert, pineapple sherbet with apricot sauce.

WINE SUGGESTION: A dry, light red wine, such as an Italian Valpolicella.

2 medium-sized eggplants, peeled	⅓ pound prosciutto ham, chopped
Salt	¼ cup heavy cream
1 tablespoon olive oil	2 tablespoons lemon juice
2 cloves garlic, minced	Olive oil for sautéing eggplant
3 cups tomatoes (if fresh, peeled and seeded; if canned, well drained)	1 cup mozzarella cheese, diced

Slice eggplants and place in a colander. Salt them lightly and leave for 1 hour to permit bitter juices to drain away.

Put 1 tablespoon olive oil in a saucepan and warm. Add garlic, let cook for a few seconds, then add tomatoes and prosciutto ham. After simmering for 1 hour, add the cream and lemon juice, stir well, and remove the mixture from heat.

Preheat oven to 350° F.

Pat eggplant slices dry with paper towels and sauté in olive oil until lightly browned.

Oil a 10-inch casserole and place a layer of eggplant slices on the bottom, overlapping them a bit. Spoon a layer of tomato sauce over the eggplant, then sprinkle half the diced mozzarella cheese over the sauce. Place the remaining eggplant on top of this, cover with the remaining mozzarella cheese and tomato sauce. You may use a smaller casserole, providing it is deep enough, and have more layers. Always start, however, with a layer of eggplant and finish with the tomato sauce.

Bake in the preheated oven for 30 minutes, covered. Uncover and bake an additional 15 minutes.

SERVES FOUR.

RATATOUILLE GRATIN
(Vegetable Mélange with Parmesan)

In contrast to the traditional way of preparing ratatouille, which calls for cooking the ingredients separately, the vegetables in this recipe are arranged in layers, with grated Parmesan cheese between them, and cooked briefly all at once.

This is really a summer-into-late-fall dish because it calls for all those vegetables which flourish under warm, blue skies. It is practically a meal in itself on a hot noon in July or August and needs little more accompaniment than a good crusty loaf of

French bread, a buttery Époisse cheese, and a chilled white wine, such as an Alsatian Sylvaner or California Chenin Blanc.

It also makes a sumptuous dinner dish, serving as both vegetable and salad. In this role, it could accompany a veal roast. For dessert, a chocolate mousse.

WINE SUGGESTION: A fruity, young red wine, such as a French Moulin-à-Vent or California Gamay Beaujolais with the veal.

Salt	1 clove garlic, minced
1 medium-sized eggplant, peeled and thinly sliced	Juice of 1 lemon
4 tablespoons olive oil	2 tablespoons fresh basil, chopped
1 large onion, thinly sliced	2 small zucchini, cut into thin rounds
1¼ cups Parmesan cheese, grated	1 large green pepper, cut into 1-inch strips
3 medium-sized tomatoes, peeled, seeded, and sliced	

Before assembling this dish, salt eggplant slices and place in a colander, weighted, for 1 hour, so they can divest themselves of their bitter juices. When the hour has passed, wipe the eggplant slices with a paper towel, and you are ready to begin composing the ratatouille.

You will need a 10-by-2-inch flame-proof baking dish. Put one tablespoon of the olive oil in the baking dish and roll the pan so oil coats the surface. Place an overlapping layer of eggplant slices on the bottom and sides of the pan. Next, place a layer of onion slices and sprinkle with Parmesan cheese. A layer of tomatoes tops this. Sprinkle half of the minced garlic, juice from half the lemon, and all the chopped basil over the layer of tomatoes.

All the zucchini slices go on top of the tomatoes with another thin layer of Parmesan cheese. Any remaining eggplant slices should be portioned out on top of the zucchini. Another layer of onions goes over the zucchini and eggplant and a final layer of tomatoes on top of the onions. Toss remaining garlic over the tomatoes and squeeze the juice from the remaining lemon half over the top layer. Place green pepper strips around the perimeter of the dish, pushing down, if necessary. Add another good coating of Parmesan cheese over the top, cover, and cook over low-to-medium heat for 20 minutes. The dish should cook at a low bubble during this time. After 20 minutes, remove from heat and carefully pour off any liquid that has accrued. Now cover the top of the dish with the remaining Parmesan cheese, giving it a thick coating, and drizzle the remaining 3 tablespoons of olive oil over the cheese. Place under broiler until the cheese has browned nicely.

You can make this version of ratatouille with less layers—or more—but it is well to remember that this dish basically cooks in the liquids rendered by many of its ingredients, notably the onions and peppers. Also, the flavors of the lemon juice and garlic are absorbed, and, in the process, heighten the flavor of the fresh vegetables.

SERVES FOUR.

FINOCCHIO ALLA FORMAGGIO
(Fennel Glazed with Cheese)

Fennel, beloved by Italians for its crisp, celerylike texture and anise flavor when eaten raw, metamorphoses into a delightfully different texture and flavor when braised in a rich stock, then gratinéed with lemon, butter, and Gruyère cheese.

The strong anise flavor that many adore, as in Pernod and other absinthe-flavored liqueurs, but which some find overpowering, is tamed in the cooking process by the lemon juice. The texture, while still pleasingly crunchy, is more tender and luscious.

Prepared this way, fennel makes a light but satisfying first course and a delectably different vegetable to serve with a grilled porterhouse steak garnished with sautéed mushrooms and buttered Belgian carrots, flecked with snipped fresh dill. Start the meal with a thin slice of silken chicken-liver pâté and a few cornichons. For dessert, small squares of double chocolate cake topped with a lavish spoonful of whipped cream spiked with a little Mirabelle plum brandy, accompanied by cups of hot, black espresso.

WINE SUGGESTION: A bold, gutsy red wine, such as an Italian Barolo or Brunello di Montalcino.

2 large fennel
2 cups rich beef stock or broth
    (see page 194)
Salt and freshly ground
    pepper to taste

½ cup lemon juice
4 slices of butter, each
    ⅛-inch thick
½ cup Gruyère cheese,
    freshly grated

Preheat oven to 350° F.

Wash fennel and slice through stems leaving about 1 inch above the bulbous root. Trim off any feathery green leaves. Scrape bulbs lightly with a vegetable peeler and trim bottoms.

Slice each bulb in half the long way and place in a saucepan that will hold them in one layer. Cover with stock. If the bulbs are not completely covered, add water. Bring to a boil, lower heat, cover, and simmer for 20 minutes until the fennel is tender but still firm. Drain, reserving ½ cup broth, and transfer the vegetable to a shallow, buttered, oven-proof dish. Season with salt and freshly ground pepper. Pour lemon juice equally over the 4 halves and pour the ½ cup reserved broth around the bulbs. Place 1 square of butter on each bulb and sprinkle with grated cheese.

Bake in the preheated oven, uncovered, for 25 minutes. The cheese should be melted, bubbly, and golden. If it isn't, run the dish under the broiler for a few minutes, but watch it carefully. Serve at once.

SERVES FOUR.

PARSNIPS GLAZED WITH LEMON AND VODKA

Vodka, lemon juice, and butter blend with the natural sweetness of parsnips and turn what some consider a lowly soup vegetable into an epicurean dish. Rounds or ovals look pretty on the plate and make a fine garniture for sliced, braised beef or roast duckling. Start the meal with wedges of chilled cantaloupe. For dessert, squares of airy sponge cake topped with a dark and bitter chocolate sauce.

WINE SUGGESTION: An assertive, mouth-filling red wine with the braised beef, such as a Côtes du Rhone from France or an Italian Gattinara.

1 pound fresh, firm young
    parsnips
Water to cover
4 tablespoons butter
½ cup vodka
⅓ cup lemon juice

1 teaspoon sugar
Salt and freshly ground
    pepper to taste
4 tablespoons fresh dill,
    finely chopped

Peel parsnips with a vegetable peeler and cut off the "tails," if there are any. Cut into rounds or ovals about ¾-inch thick. Place in a saucepan, cover with cold water, and bring to a boil. Lower heat and simmer for 6 to 8 minutes; parsnips should still be firm. Drain in a colander.

Melt the butter in a skillet and add the drained parsnips. Pour vodka over the parsnips and cook for a few minutes over medium heat, shaking the pan to dissipate the alcohol. Lower heat to simmer and add lemon juice, sugar, salt and pepper, and cook, uncovered, 5 to 10 minutes, shaking the pan occasionally. When the juices have reduced and the parsnips are nicely glazed, turn them into a heated serving bowl and sprinkle with chopped dill.

SERVES FOUR.

SPINACH PUREE IN ARTICHOKE BOTTOMS

Sautéed bacon contributes a smoky flavor to this delicious purée which, when spooned into little artichoke bottoms and topped with a splash of whipped cream, can garnish almost anything from roast pork or filet mignon to a simple cheese omelet.

1 pound fresh spinach
4 slices bacon
3 small shallots, chopped
2 tablespoons lemon juice
¼ teaspoon salt

8 small artichoke bottoms,
canned or freshly
cooked
½ cup heavy cream,
whipped

Wash spinach thoroughly to rid it of the sand that seems to im-pregnate each curly leaf. The best way to do this is to fill a large container with cold water and plunge the spinach up and down in the water. Lift spinach out and place in a colander; pour water out of container, refill, and wash spinach again. You may have to do this several times.

Next, fold each spinach leaf inward and pull off the stem and spine. Set spinach aside.

Sauté bacon and, when crisp, remove slices to absorbent toweling. Add chopped shallots to the hot bacon grease, cook for a couple of seconds, then add spinach and toss thoroughly until slightly wilted and coated with the bacon grease. Put spinach, bacon, shallots, lemon juice, and salt in a blender or food proc-essor and purée.

Spoon the purée into 8 small, cooked artichoke bottoms and top with unsweetened whipped cream.

SERVES FOUR.

CABBAGE AU GRATIN

This is a great fresh cabbage dish from the distinguished dean of American cookery, James Beard. The crisp texture of the shredded cabbage is a delightful contrast to the lemon-enhanced béchamel sauce, the whole gratinéed briefly in a hot oven. Serve the cabbage as an accompaniment to a robust meatloaf for a satisfying Sunday-night supper. For dessert, something refreshingly light, such as chilled cubes of casaba melon marinated in a sweet Madeira wine.

WINE SUGGESTION: A hearty California Burgundy or Mountain Red.

THE CABBAGE
 1 medium-sized head cabbage
 (about 2½ pounds)
 1 quart chicken stock (see
 page 198)

THE BÉCHAMEL SAUCE

3 tablespoons butter
3 tablespoons flour
1 cup chicken stock (reserve
 from cooking liquid)
Salt and freshly ground
 pepper to taste

1 cup light cream
3 tablespoons lemon juice
Five to six paper-thin slices
 of lemon
¼ cup Parmesan or
 Gruyère cheese,
 freshly grated

Preheat oven to 400° F.

Butter a 2-quart casserole. Wash and drain cabbage, remove all the center core, and shred as for cole slaw. Place the cabbage in a 3-quart saucepan, add chicken stock, bring to a boil, and cook, uncovered, until barely tender, about 6 minutes. Drain the cabbage, reserving the stock.

To prepare a rich cream sauce, melt the butter in a small

saucepan. Over low heat, add the flour, stirring until a smooth paste is formed, about 1 minute. Gradually add the hot reserved stock, stirring until smooth and thickened. Add salt and freshly ground pepper to taste. Add the cream, stirring to keep the sauce smooth and creamy, and finally, add the lemon juice.

Pour the sauce over the cabbage and toss lightly with two forks to coat the shreds completely. Turn the cabbage into the buttered casserole. Top with the lemon slices and cover with grated cheese. Place in the preheated oven for 10 to 15 minutes, until lightly brown on top.

SERVES FOUR.

ZUCCHINI GRATINEE

Zucchini is a many-faceted vegetable. It's lovely sautéed and tossed with hot pasta; steamed, it can go alone, with just a little butter dressing, or it can be mixed into a bowl of fluffy rice; and it provides texture contrast in a salad of mixed greens. Here, it's affinity for cheese becomes apparent.

In this recipe, the meat of the zucchini is mixed with a blend of sautéed shallots and lemon pulp, piled back into the scooped-out zucchini boats, topped with cheese, and placed under the broiler until the cheese is lightly browned.

Serve the zucchini with broiled chicken breasts and small, baked potatoes. The first course could be cold, poached salmon with a green mayonnaise sauce. For dessert, crème aux amandes, a custard made with heavy cream and very little sugar and served with toasted almonds.

WINE SUGGESTION: A not-too-dry white California varietal, such as a Chenin Blanc or French Colombard.

> 5 medium-sized zucchini, about 1½ pounds
> 1 tablespoon butter
> 2 small shallots, peeled and finely minced
> Pulp of 1 lemon
> Gruyère cheese

Trim the ends off the zucchini. Cut each in half and then slice each half horizontally. With a sharp knife cut out the soft center part—follow the line of the little transparent seeds. Chop the meat coarsely and set aside.

Melt the butter in a skillet and add the minced shallots. Peel the lemon, making sure the white pith is removed. Cut out the lemon segments, and cut the segments into pieces. Add to the shallots and butter and cook gently for a few minutes. Turn off heat and stir in the chopped zucchini meat. Mix well and set aside.

In a pot large enough to accommodate the 20 little zucchini boats covered with water, first bring the water to a brisk boil. Turn off heat, put the zucchini boats into the hot water, and let stand for 5 minutes; then drain in a colander and rinse with cold water to stop the cooking. The zucchini boats should be tender but still firm. Pat the boats dry and distribute the zucchini-lemon mixture among the boats. Top each with a slice or two of Gruyère cheese.

At this point, the dish can wait several hours. When ready to serve, slide the zucchini under the broiler until the cheese is golden brown.

Parmesan cheese may be used instead of the Gruyère. If you use Parmesan, layer it on the zucchini thickly and dot with butter before placing under the broiler. The butter keeps the Parmesan cheese moist.

SERVES FOUR.

SAUTEED CARROTS

While fingers of raw carrots make undeniably good munching, and tiny new carrots take well to a brief boil and sweet butter, one of the best ways to prepare carrots year-round is to sauté them —somehow it gives them more character. In this recipe, carrot slices are browned slowly in butter, then tossed with minced shallots and lemon juice until glazed.

Serve them with pork chops braised with onions and herbs and a small, leafy salad. For dessert, an apple tart.

WINE SUGGESTION: A fruity red wine, such as a California Gamay Beaujolais.

1 pound carrots, cut into
½-inch rounds
2 tablespoons butter
1 teaspoon salt

2 tablespoons shallots, minced
3 tablespoons lemon juice
Freshly ground pepper to taste

Sauté the carrots in melted butter over medium heat, stirring occasionally so they will cook evenly. When browned and almost tender, about 15 minutes, add shallots and 2 tablespoons of the lemon juice. Continue cooking and tossing the carrots until

they are slightly glazed. Remove from heat, add salt, pepper, and
the remaining tablespoon of lemon juice.

SERVES FOUR.

CURRIED TURNIPS

Turnips, wonderful in stews or roasted along with a loin of pork,
taste quite different when steamed with yogurt, lemon juice, and
curry.

Serve these curried turnips with pork chops that have been
sautéed, then simmered in a bit of white wine. The first course
could be mussels vinaigrette. For dessert, baked apples stuffed
with chopped candied fruit and walnuts.

WINE SUGGESTION: A fruity red for the pork chops, such as a
chilled Beaujolais or a young Spanish Rioja.

2 tablespoons butter	1½ pounds turnips, peeled
1 small onion, sliced thinly	and cubed
Juice of 1 lemon	1 teaspoon salt
4 tablespoons plain yogurt	1 teaspoon curry powder

Melt butter and add sliced onions. Cook over low heat until
onions are limp and most of the butter is absorbed. Add the
lemon juice and cook for 3 minutes, or until it, too, has been
mostly absorbed. Add yogurt, stir, and continue cooking for
another 3 minutes. Add turnips and salt, and toss well. Cover and
cook over low heat for approximately 20 minutes. Check every 5
to 8 minutes, stirring each time. If the mixture seems dry, add 1

tablespoon water or stock. The turnips should be fairly dry when done, but, of course, they should not stick to the pan. When the turnips are almost tender, stir in the curry powder. Cook, covered, for another 5 minutes.

SERVES FOUR.

SWEET AND TART ONIONS

The onion is a versatile vegetable. Raw, it provides a lively addition to a garden salad; boiled and sauced with butter, it is a savory side dish. And when, as here, onions are sautéed, and then cooked gently in a lemon-sherry sauce, they are given an added taste dimension. These sweet and tart onions go especially well with roasted fowl. Serve them with a chestnut-stuffed roast turkey, boiled baby carrots tossed in butter, and brussels sprouts vinaigrette. For dessert, a Sacher torte with chocolate-cream filling.

WINE SUGGESTIONS: A full-bodied, dry white wine, such as a Chardonnay or a light red wine, such as a California Gamay Beaujolais.

3 tablespoons butter	½ cup cream sherry
2 pounds small, white onions	3 tablespoons lemon juice
1 teaspoon salt	1 tablespoon brown sugar

Melt the butter in a skillet or shallow pan large enough to accommodate the onions in a single layer. Add the onions and salt and sauté until lightly browned, turning the onions so they brown fairly evenly. This will take about 10 minutes.

Add the sherry and lemon juice and sprinkle brown sugar over the onions. Cover and cook over medium heat for 10 minutes. Uncover and continue cooking, turning the onions occasionally, until tender when pierced with the tines of a fork.

SERVES FOUR.

VARIATION

The same recipe, with fewer onions and the addition of pork chops, makes a satisfying dinner for two. Accompany it with a garden lettuce salad and follow it with peppermint ice cream and chocolate sauce.

WINE SUGGESTION: A medium-bodied, fairly robust, dry red wine, such as an Italian Spanna or California Pinot Noir.

2 tablespoons butter	½ cup cream sherry
Two 2-inch rib pork chops	3 tablespoons lemon juice
6 small, white onions	1 teaspoon salt

Melt the butter in a skillet and add the chops and onions. Brown pork chops for 7 minutes on each side, turning the onions every now and then so that they brown as well. Add the sherry, lemon juice, and salt. Cover and simmer for 20 minutes.

SERVES TWO.

LEMON-DILL NEW POTATOES

New potatoes can accompany almost anything—broiled fish, roasts, chicken—and are good served in their jackets. They are small, convenient morsels that soak up juices or the remnants of a buttery sauce.

In our version, however, they are peeled, boiled, tossed briefly with lemon juice—which is then poured off because the steamy little potatoes absorb quickly—and then rolled in butter and fresh dill.

Made this way, the potatoes could go well with trout baked in cream and braised leeks. For dessert, an apple pudding with almonds.

WINE SUGGESTION: A light and crisp dry white wine, such as a Loire Valley Fumé Blanc, Chilean Riesling, or Alsatian Sylvaner.

12 new potatoes, peeled
3 tablespoons lemon juice
4 tablespoons butter
6 tablespoons fresh dill, minced

Boil the potatoes in a covered saucepan until tender, about 25 to 30 minutes. Test with the tines of a fork. Drain, and pour the lemon juice over the potatoes, turning them gently so each has a brief soaking in the juice. Pour the lemon juice off, add butter, and toss carefully so the potatoes are well coated. Place in a serving dish and sprinkle the dill over all.

SERVES FOUR.

DESSERTS

COLD LEMON NOUGATINE SOUFFLE

A cold lemon soufflé is one of the loveliest desserts in the world. This version has no gelatin and is made by simply cooking egg yolks with lemon and sugar until thick, folding in nougatine and egg whites, and then chilling.

It is light and lemony and, with the delicate trace of nougatine throughout, uttterly delicious. It can also be made very quickly, if you have prepared the nougatine ahead of time and if everything else is right. For instance, the eggs really must be at room temperature in order to be whipped quickly with a hand mixer at high speed.

This dessert could follow almost any meal but is especially nice after a substantial entrée or a very spicy one, such as chicken curry (see page 83). Since the curry is accompanied by several condiments, all you might need in addition would be a green salad and a light first course, such as celery à la Grecque.

WINE SUGGESTION: Most wines are overpowered by the strong flavors of the curry. A well-chilled beer is the best choice, or serve a light, medium-dry white wine, such as German Liebfraumilch.

> 7 egg yolks
> ¾ cup sugar
> ½ cup lemon juice
> 4 tablespoons nougatine (recipe follows)
> 7 egg whites

Beat the egg yolks with a whisk in the top of a double boiler (see Note), off the heat, until light. Add sugar and lemon juice and beat briefly. Place over simmering water and cook, stirring constantly with a whisk, until the mixture is quite thick.

Once the lemon-egg-yolk combination is thick, remove from heat and let it cool. Placing it in the freezer for about 5 minutes will bring it to the right temperature. While it is cooling, whip the egg whites until they hold a peak when the beater is removed. Do not let them become too stiff or it will be difficult to fold them into the lemon mixture.

Stir the nougatine into the cooled lemon-yolk mixture and then fold in the beaten egg whites thoroughly, using a spatula and turning the bowl as you fold to make sure everything is well mixed. Pour into a 2-quart soufflé dish and refrigerate at least 1 hour.

SERVES SIX TO EIGHT.

Note: Do not use an aluminum double boiler or pan because aluminum causes egg yolks to discolor. In lieu of a double boiler, any pan may be used, assuming you have another container into which it will fit. There should not be a lot of water in the base container, and the water should never touch the bottom of the pan containing the egg-yolk mixture. What you want is steam. It is best to bring the water in the bottom of the double boiler (or whatever container you are using) to a boil and then lower heat when you put the container with the egg-yolk mixture in place.

NOUGATINE

½ cup almonds, slivered and toasted
½ cup sugar
2 tablespoons water

Preheat oven to 350° F.

To toast the almonds, spread evenly in a pan and place in the preheated oven for about 10 minutes, or until lightly browned, then cool.

Combine sugar and water in a small saucepan and stir off the heat until the sugar is dissolved. If you don't do this, you will end up with a solid block of sugar crystals.

Once dissolved, place over medium heat and boil gently, without stirring, until the sugar turns golden. Watch this carefully; if the sugar becomes too dark, the syrup will be bitter. It should be a light caramel color. When it reaches this stage, add almonds immediately, stir, and pour the mixture onto a sheet of oiled waxed paper. Let it cool, break into chunks, and pulverize in the blender. MAKES ABOUT ¾ CUP.

Note: It's possible to double the above recipe, but it takes so long to dissolve the sugar, and then for it to turn golden, that it is really quicker to make two batches in the above amounts. Nougatine keeps indefinitely when refrigerated in a covered jar and can be used on ice cream and in other desserts.

LEMON SPONGE PUDDING

This is a spectacular dessert. When finished, it has a topping that is a cross between the lightest of sponge cakes and a meringue and it seemingly melts into the creamy, fluffy base. It is so incredibly easy to make the result seems even more extraordinary.

Precede it with tiny bay scallops, sautéed in butter, and ratatouille gratin (see page 134). A nice first course would be pâté en croute with a good French mustard.

WINE SUGGESTION: A crisp white wine, such as Saint Véran or Pouilly Fumé.

3 extra large eggs, separated	1 cup sugar
½ cup heavy cream	4 tablespoons lemon juice
3 tablespoons flour	¼ teaspoon cream of tartar

Preheat oven to 350° F.

Beat the egg yolks and the cream together with a spoon, and sift the flour and sugar into the mixture. Add the lemon juice and mix lightly. Whip the egg whites until foamy, add cream of tartar, and continue to beat the egg whites until they hold their shape.

Without washing the whisk or hand mixer used to whip the egg whites, whip the egg-yolk-cream mixture until it is perfectly smooth and very pale in color. Now fold in the egg whites and pour into a buttered baking dish, 4-by-7 inches—a 1-quart soufflé dish is perfect. Set in larger container, pour boiling water to reach halfway up the soufflé dish and bake in the preheated oven for 45 minutes. The top of the finished pudding will be a pale brown.

SERVES THREE TO FOUR.

CHOCOLATE MOUSSE WITH LEMON LIQUEUR

The addition of lemon liqueur to this chocolate mousse infuses it with a subtle perfume. It's not instantly identifiable, but it makes the rich mousse even more luxurious.

Precede the mousse with chicken breasts that have been stuffed with ricotta cheese, garlic, and spinach and artichoke bottoms filled with a basil-flavored tomato purée.

WINE SUGGESTION: A Gamay Beaujolais from California.

> 4 ounces sweet, dark chocolate
> 2 ounces unsweetened chocolate
> 7 tablespoons lemon liqueur
> 5 eggs, separated

Lightly butter a saucepan—this helps insure that the chocolate will not burn. Put sweet and unsweetened chocolate in the saucepan over low heat. As it starts to melt add 5 tablespoons of the lemon liqueur. When the chocolate is completely melted, add the egg yolks, one at a time, mixing well after each addition. Remove from heat and add the remaining 2 tablespoons of lemon liqueur.

Beat the egg whites until they hold soft peaks and fold thoroughly into the chocolate mixture. Make sure there are no little globules of egg white in the mousse. Pour into a 2-quart soufflé dish and refrigerate for at least 2 hours.

SERVES FOUR.

BAKED LEMON SOUFFLE

A light cake topping conceals a creamy, thick lemon base in this unusual version of a soufflé. Serve it after a beef en daube (see page 109) that has been cooked with turnips, carrots, and leeks. The first course could be slices of duck pâté with cornichon pickles.

WINE SUGGESTION: A sturdy, earthy, dry red wine with the beef, such as a New York State Baco Noir.

1½ cups sugar	⅓ cup lemon juice
¼ pound butter, melted	½ cup sifted flour
4 eggs, separated	1 cup milk

Preheat oven to 375° F.

Add sugar to the melted butter and mix well. Beat egg yolks and add to the butter-sugar mixture, along with the lemon juice. Again, mix well. Add flour alternately with milk, beating after each addition, making sure the mixture is smooth.

Whip the egg whites until stiff and fold them into the lemon-yolk mixture. Pour into oiled, 2-quart soufflé dish and place in a water bath—a container large enough to hold the soufflé dish filled with enough water to come one-third of the way outside the soufflé dish. Bake in the preheated oven for about 1 hour; the top will be lightly brown. Cool and serve at room temperature or chilled.

SERVES SIX TO EIGHT.

THE PERFECT LEMON MERINGUE PIE

We think our version of this pie is the best we have ever tasted. There is no cornstarch or gelatin in it, and, when done, it is fluffy, light, and delicious. The crust is thin, crisp, and faintly sweet; the lemon filling is especially light because beaten egg whites are folded into it; and the meringue itself is baked so briefly that it remains wonderfully tender.

Precede this pie with escalopes of veal that have been lightly browned, then cooked briefly in a little veal stock and wine. A spinach salad with sliced raw mushrooms and fried, crumbled bacon would complement the veal nicely.

WINE SUGGESTION: A light, crisp white wine, such as an Alsatian Riesling.

THE FLAKY PIECRUST
   ¾ cup flour
   3 tablespoons confectioners' sugar
   7 tablespoons butter (1 tablespoon less than ¼ pound)
   1 extra large egg
   1 tablespoon ice water, if needed

THE LEMON FILLING
            7 eggs, separated
            1 cup plus 2 tablespoons sugar
            ⅓ cup lemon juice

Preheat oven to 350° F.
   To prepare the crust, place flour and sugar in a bowl. Cut

butter, which must be very cold, into bits and add to the flour-sugar mixture. A quick way to cut the butter into bits is to first remove from the ¼-pound of butter, the 1 tablespoon you will not be using. Then slice the rectangle of butter that's left 3 times, lengthwise; turn it on its side and slice it again lengthwise. Then cut across the bar crosswise. You will end up with lots of little squares. Toss these into the flour and, using a pastry cutter or 2 knives held together in one hand, cut the butter into the flour until the mixture is the texture of meal.

Break the whole egg into the mixture and, using a long-tined fork, beat it well into the flour. Add the ice water if necessary to make the pastry more manageable. Form the dough into a ball and place it on lightly floured waxed paper. Knead mildly with the heel of your hand to insure that the butter is well incorporated. Form into a ball again, dust lightly with flour, and wrap in waxed paper. Refrigerate for at least 1 hour.

Roll the chilled dough on a lightly floured surface to ⅛-inch thickness. Flip it over the rolling pin and place it into a pie plate, fitting the dough gently into place. Trim excess, leaving a ¼-inch overhang. Press or pinch the overhang decoratively.

Line the shell with aluminum foil and fill the foil with dried beans. Place in the preheated oven for 15 minutes. Carefully remove the foil from the pie crust, prick the bottom of the shell with the tines of a fork, and return to the oven for 10 minutes more, or until lightly colored. Save the dried beans; you can keep them almost indefinitely and re-use them every time you make a pie crust.

Some notes on this pie crust recipe:

Use only butter for the best-tasting pie crust. The addition of vegetable shortening in any form invariably distorts the taste.

The addition of sugar makes this crust, when baked, like a thin, delicate cooky and is very nice with fruit or fruit-flavored fillings. Without the sugar, this makes a crust suitable for any filling.

Preheat oven to 350° F.

To prepare the lemon filling, you will need a double boiler (never an aluminum one—it discolors the eggs) or a pan that will fit snugly into another without touching the bottom. Beat the egg yolks with a whisk in the top of the double boiler, off the heat. Add the 1 cup of sugar and the lemon juice and beat again, briefly. Place over a container of simmering water. Cook, stirring constantly, until the mixture is quite thick. Remove from heat and cool.

Beat egg whites until they hold soft peaks. Incorporate approximately one-third of the egg whites into the lemon mixture, using a spatula and mixing thoroughly. Pour into the baked pie crust. Add the remaining 2 tablespoons of sugar to the remaining egg whites, one at a time, beating after each addition. When the egg whites are glossy, but not overly stiff, pile onto the lemon filling, covering it completely. You can do this by using a wide, large spoon to scoop up the egg whites and drop them onto the filling. The meringue should look fluffy, like puffy clouds.

Place the pie in the preheated oven for no more than 10 minutes, or until the meringue is very lightly browned.

SERVES SIX.

UN SUSURRO DOLCE
(Poached Meringue)

In Italian, *un susurro* is a whisper, and that's what this gossamer poached meringue is—just a whisper of something delicate and sweet after a substantial meal. Tiny golden threads of lemon zest add color and tartness to a snowlike mound of beaten egg whites baked in a *bain-marie*—water bath—until puffed and lightly golden on top. This susurro may be served at room temperature, when its texture is the lightest, or chilled for several hours in the refrigerator, which will firm, but not toughen the texture. We like to scoop it right from the soufflé dish into individual glass saucers and pass a bowl of puréed red-ripe strawberries. As an alternate and for a more elaborate presentation, the meringue can be baked in a ring mold, cooled, unmolded, and the center filled with fresh strawberries.

Start the meal with a fine chicken-liver pâté served with thin, hot toast. The entrée is duckling, cut into quarters, pricked with the tines of a fork to permit the fat to run off, dusted with fresh pepper, and roasted in a hot oven until crisp and succulent. Serve the duckling with a mixture of long grain and wild rice, cooked together in chicken stock until dry and fluffy. As a salad course, cut endive into thin circles, toss with chopped scallions and a little oil and lemon juice.

WINE SUGGESTION: A fruity red wine, such as an Italian Bardolino or a fine French Beaujolais.

4 extra large egg whites	2 teaspoons lemon juice
A pinch of salt	1 cup ripe strawberries,
½ cup sugar, scant	puréed
3 teaspoons lemon zest, grated into threads	

Preheat oven to 325° F.

Lightly butter a 1-quart soufflé mold or ring mold. Have ready a larger pan that will hold water to three-quarters the depth of the soufflé dish. Break the egg whites into a deep bowl, add the pinch of salt, and beat with an electric mixer until foamy but not stiff. Gradually add the sugar, beating until the whites are stiff enough to hold peaks. Lightly fold in the grated lemon zest and the lemon juice. Turn the mixture into the buttered soufflé dish or ring mold, set dish in the larger pan, and fill it with water to three-fourths the depth of the dish holding the egg-white mixture. Bake from 30 to 40 minutes, or until the top is lightly golden. The meringue will puff up, like a soufflé, but will deflate as it cools. Cool the sussuro on a cake rack and serve at room temperature. Or cool and then refrigerate until ready to serve. The susurro is best served the same day, but it will keep overnight in the refrigerator, loosely covered.

SERVES FOUR.

LEMON ANGEL PIE

A perfectly baked meringue shell makes a delightful change in taste and texture from the usual pie crusts. When filled with a rich, lemony custard, it becomes a very special dessert.

Just make sure you make the meringue shell on a dry day; damp weather defeats a crisp meringue.

This dessert would make a nice conclusion to a meal that starts with onion soup flavored with Calvados apple brandy, followed by sweetbreads in a port wine and cream sauce, and buttered baby green beans.

WINE SUGGESTION: A light, dry red wine, such as a California Ruby Cabernet or a Bordeaux Supérieur.

THE MERINGUE SHELL

> 2 egg whites
> 1 teaspoon cream of tartar
> Scant ½ cup of sugar

THE FILLING

> 4 egg yolks
> 1 cup sugar
> ½ cup lemon juice
> ¼ pound butter, cut into 4 pieces

Preheat oven to 300° F.

Whip the egg whites until foamy and add the cream of tartar. Continue beating the egg whites until soft peaks form. Add sugar, a little at a time, beating well after each addition. When all the sugar is incorporated, the egg whites should be glossy and fairly stiff. With a spatula, spread the egg whites onto a buttered, 9-inch pie plate, bringing the meringue up around the edges to form a shell. Bake in the preheated oven for about 1 hour, but be sure to check the meringue after 50 minutes. It should feel dry when done and not sticky, and it may take another 10 minutes to reach this consistency.

Prepare the filling while the meringue is baking. In the top of a double boiler, or its equivalent, beat the egg yolks, sugar, and lemon juice until light in color. Place the mixture over barely simmering water and, stirring or whisking constantly, add pieces of butter, waiting until each piece has melted before adding the next. Continue stirring until the mixture is quite thick. Remove from heat and continue stirring until the mixture cools somewhat.

It may be refrigerated until you are ready to pour it into the meringue shell. As it cools, the filling thickens even more. Whisk or beat it again before pouring it into the meringue. The pie may be served at room temperature or it may be chilled.

SERVES FOUR TO SIX.

TARTE CITRON MAMA
(Almond Lemon Tart)

André Soltner, chef-owner of the famous Lutèce restaurant in New York, gave us the recipe for this charming little cake with its moist, almond-impregnated base topped by a layer of lemon slices and a thin meringue.

The recipe came to Soltner from a patron whose family had been making the cake since the twelfth century, passing it down from mother to daughter, hence the name "mama."

It is a delightful dessert due partially to the juxtaposition of sweet and tart flavors and the pleasant mingling of textures. It could be the conclusion to almost any kind of meal from simple to complex. As a happy medium, we suggest it be preceded by grilled turbot seasoned with tarragon, fresh spinach that has been washed and tossed briefly in melted butter and a bit of lemon juice, and a light, saffron-flavored risotto.

The cake alone is perfect with a chilled glass of French Sauternes.

WINE SUGGESTION: With the turbot, a big, full-bodied white wine, such as a California Chardonnay.

THE BASE

> 3 extra large eggs, separated
> ¾ cup sugar
> Grated peel of 1 lemon
> 1 cup almonds, finely ground
> 1 tablespoon flour

THE TOPPING

> 2 lemons, peeled and sliced thinly
> 2 egg whites
> ¼ cup sugar
> ¾ cup almonds, finely ground

Preheat oven to 350° F.

Beat the egg yolks and sugar until very pale and the mixture falls from the whisk in a ribbon. Then add the lemon peel and mix. Add ground almonds and flour. Beat egg whites until stiff and fold into batter.

Butter a 9-inch pie plate or tart tin and pour in the batter. Bake in the preheated oven for about 30 minutes, or until the cake is lightly browned.

While cake is baking, prepare the topping. Peel and slice lemons; remove the cake from the oven and cover with lemon slices, overlapping them slightly.

Beat egg whites until they reach soft peaks, then add sugar in increments, beating after each addition. Fold in the ground almonds and spread the meringue over the lemon slices, using a spatula dipped in cold water. Return the cake to the oven for about 15 minutes.

SERVES SIX.

LEMON SPONGE CAKE

The two keys to a fine-textured, airy sponge cake are a light
hand in folding in the egg whites and an oven that's on the cool
side, 325° F. We like the taste of lemon in the sponge cake and
the contrast of a golden crisp crust and feathery-textured interior.
It's wonderful served plain at tea or coffee time; it takes well to a
dusting of confectioners' sugar or lemon icing and becomes posi-
tively festive with a topping of lightly sweetened whipped cream
and a scoop of fresh blueberries, or any berries for that matter.

Plain slices of sponge cake are especially appropriate after a
sturdy entrée, such as corned beef braised with green cabbage
and garnished with new potatoes bathed in chive-scented melted
butter.

WINE SUGGESTION: A New York State Chancellor or Baco
Noir, or a California Zinfandel.

8 large eggs, separated
A pinch of salt
1 cup superfine granulated sugar
⅓ cup fresh lemon juice
1 cup cake flour sifted 3 times, then measured again to make 1 cup

Preheat oven to 325° F.

Have all the ingredients at room temperature. This is especially important to prevent the lemon juice from curdling the
egg yolks and to insure that the egg whites will beat up to a
fluffier consistency. Use 2 large mixing bowls. Separate the eggs,

dropping the yolks into one, the whites into the other. Add the pinch of salt to the whites. Using an electric beater, beat the yolks until they're lemon colored and thickened. Gradually add the sugar, continuing to beat until well blended and smooth. Add the lemon juice and beat until blended. Set aside. Wash and thoroughly dry your beaters before whipping the egg whites, which should be beaten until they are stiff enough to hold firm peaks. Shake off any excess whites that cling to your beater. Use a large, slotted spoon and quickly fold half the egg whites into the egg-yolk mixture, folding just until the whites disappear. Sift in the cake flour, carefully folding it into the batter. Lastly, add the remaining beaten egg whites, using as few strokes as possible. Use a plastic or rubber spatula to turn the batter into an ungreased 8-inch tube pan and bake for 1 hour. The cake should be golden brown with the sides pulling away from the tin. Invert onto a rack until the cake is cool, then remove from the pan.

The sponge cake keeps best if placed on a plate with a fairly loose draping of aluminum foil around and over it. Don't wrap it tightly in foil or plastic wrap, as this will cause the delicate crisp crust to become soggy. Sponge cake is not for keeping, so plan to use it within 2 days.

SERVES EIGHT TO TEN.

MADEIRA LEMON CAKE

Madeira and lemon juice glaze a lusciously light cake while it's still fragrantly warm from the oven. The top of the cake is pronged with the tines of a fork to allow the glaze to seep down into it, adding aromatic flavor and additional moisture to the texture. This makes a very special tea- or coffee-time accompaniment and is also an enchanting dessert to serve after a substantial entrée, such as carbonnade of beef.

WINE SUGGESTION: Beer is the traditional beverage to enjoy with carbonnade, which is itself prepared with beer.

THE CAKE
  ½ pound sweet butter
  Grated rind of 2 lemons
  1 cup sugar
  4 eggs
  2 cups flour sifted with 2 teaspoons baking powder
      and ¼ teaspoon salt

THE GLAZE
  1 cup sifted confectioners' sugar
  ½ cup lemon juice
  ½ cup dry Madeira (Rainwater or Sercial)

Preheat oven to 350° F.

Cream the butter, lemon rind, and sugar until light and fluffy. Beat in the eggs, one at a time, until well blended, then add the sifted flour, baking powder, and salt, stirring just until the flour disappears. Pour batter into a lightly greased 9-inch-round cake tin, and bake 25 to 35 minutes, or until the top is golden. Place cake on a cooling rack, and with a fork, prick the top of the cake liberally. After mixing the glaze ingredients together until smooth and quite liquid, spoon the glaze over the top of the cake. Permit the cake to stand at room temperature several hours before serving. Since this is a moist cake, it will keep for 4 or 5 days if covered well.

SERVES SIX TO EIGHT.

LEMON CHEESECAKE

Light, moist, and creamy, with just the right degree of tartness, this cheesecake is especially delightful with after-theater coffee or other late-evening repasts, or as a dessert after a not-too-heavy Sunday supper. The cake will keep in the refrigerator for a week —if you can keep it that long. The crust is thin and delicate because the zweibach crumbs are not, as in some recipes, blended with butter and sugar to a heavy consistency, which makes it even more simple to prepare. Just butter the tin, dust it with the fine crumbs, and shake briskly to distribute them as evenly as possible.

The proportions below are for a 9- to 10-inch cheesecake pan, which will provide 20 slices or more. For a smaller size, use a 7-inch pan and halve the ingredients, using 3 tablespoons of lemon juice.

1 cup zweibach crumbs, finely pulverized	1 cup heavy sweet cream, unwhipped
2½ pounds cream cheese	⅓ cup lemon juice
2½ cups sugar	Grated rind of 1 lemon,
6 extra large eggs	optional

Preheat oven to 450° F.

Lightly butter a 9- or 10-inch springform pan. Sprinkle the bottom and sides with the zweibach crumbs and shake to distribute evenly.

Have all the ingredients at room temperature. Cream the

cheese until soft. Add sugar gradually and beat with an electric beater or heavy wooden spoon until well blended. Add the eggs, one at a time, mixing well. Blend the cream and lemon juice into the mixture. Pour batter into prepared springform pan and bake in the preheated oven for 10 minutes, no longer. Reduce heat to 350° F., and bake the cake 50 minutes to 1 hour, or until the top is golden brown and the center is no longer soft. When done, turn off heat and leave the cake in the oven with the door closed for 1 hour longer. Cool. Remove from pan and store in the refrigerator.

SERVES TWENTY.

IRISH SEED CAKE

Crisp caraway seeds and grated lemon rind lace this finely textured cake. It is nice sliced and warmed for breakfast with English gooseberry jam, a big pot of Viennese coffee, and a pitcher of heavy cream, or at teatime with a brisk Earl Gray tea. It's one of those cakes that can be served any time of day, and it keeps well. It must be baked in a pan with a center tube.

1 cup butter (½ pound)	1 teaspoon baking powder
1 cup sugar	3 tablespoons caraway seeds
4 eggs, separated	Grated rind of 2 large
1½ cups flour	lemons

Preheat oven to 350° F.

Cream butter and sugar together until pale; then add the egg yolks and beat well. Gradually add flour, baking powder, cara-

way seeds, and lemon rind. Fold in well-beaten egg whites, blending thoroughly. Pour the batter into a buttered tube pan. Bake in the preheated oven for a half-hour, reduce heat to 300° F., and continue baking for another half-hour. Remove the cake from the oven—it should be lightly browned—and let it sit for a few minutes. When the cake has cooled slightly, loosen it from the sides of the pan and around the tube, and turn out onto a platter.
SERVES EIGHT TO TEN.

LEMON TUILES
(Almond Lemon Cookies)

Our version of this classic French cooky—whose name derives from the curvy French roof tiles its shape emulates—has grated lemon peel in addition to the almonds, unbeaten egg whites, and sugar that give it such a thin, crisp consistency.

There's hardly any time or place that these delicate cookies cannot be served, and, packed carefully in a pretty tin, they make a delicious gift.

Some recipes for tuiles call for the butter and sugar to be creamed. We have found, however, that melting the butter makes for a finer-textured cookie. Also, since the batter is thin, be sure to butter *and flour* your cookie sheet. If it is just buttered, the batter tends to slide and run together.

2 egg whites, unbeaten
⅓ cup sugar
4 tablespoons melted butter, cooled

3 tablespoons flour
½ cup slivered almonds
1 tablespoon lemon rind, finely grated

Preheat oven to 375° F.

Mix the unbeaten egg whites and sugar together, and add cooled, melted butter. Mix well and beat in the flour. Add almonds and lemon rind and stir until well mixed. Drop by spoonfuls onto a buttered and floured cookie sheet, about 2 inches apart. Bake in the preheated oven for approximately 10 minutes or until the cookies are slightly brown around the edges. Remove from the oven, and with a metal spatula or knife, carefully slide cookies off and hang them over a broomstick handle, much the way you would hang a doily on a clothesline (see Note). This is what gives them their traditional shape. They crisp quickly on the broomstick handle and can then be removed easily.

If the cookies start to harden on the cooky sheet while you're in the process of removing them, pop them back into the oven for a few seconds and they will soften again.

MAKES ABOUT TWENTY-FIVE TUILES.

Note: If you don't have a broomstick or mop handle readily available, you can use a rolling pin or bottles. However, the broomstick handle is ideal, since you can hang a lot of tuiles on it at once, so you might consider borrowing someone's broom.

LEMON SQUARES

A shortbreadlike base and a moist, lemony top make these cookies similar to little tarts. They can be made quickly and tend to disappear quickly. Serve them with sherry on a wintry Sunday afternoon when there's a good fire going in the fireplace, or think of them as a light, tart-sweet summer dessert to follow a salad of baby bibb lettuce, tuna, and black olives.

1 cup flour	2 eggs
¼ cup confectioners' sugar	1 cup sugar
¼ pound sweet butter	Juice of 2 lemons

Preheat oven to 325° F.

Mix the flour and confectioners' sugar and cut in the butter. Combine until pebbly and pat into an 8-inch square pan. Bake in the preheated oven for 20 minutes.

Meanwhile, beat the 2 eggs until quite pale. Add sugar and continue beating until mixture is thick and cream colored. Then beat in the lemon juice.

When the base pastry is done, remove from the oven and raise heat to 350° F. Pour the egg mixture over the base and return to the oven for 20 minutes.

MAKES SIXTEEN SQUARES.

GINGERED LEMON COOKIES

You won't taste the lemon in these soft, not-too-sweet gingery cookies, but the fresh lemon juice enhances the ginger flavor and cuts the cloying qualities of the molasses. They match nicely with fruit desserts and ice cream. We like them with steaming, freshly brewed tea on a cold winter evening. A youngster we know loves them with a tart, crisp lady apple after school.

Grated rind of 1 lemon	1 egg, lightly beaten
½ cup sugar	½ cup dark molasses
½ pound sweet butter, softened	4 tablespoons lemon juice
	2 cups sifted flour

⅛ teaspoon salt

2 teaspoons baking soda

1 tablespoon powdered
ginger

Preheat oven to 350° F.

Mix the grated lemon rind and the sugar thoroughly; then add the softened butter and cream well. Beat in the egg until blended. Stir in the molasses and lemon juice and mix well. Sift together flour, salt, baking soda, and ginger and add this to the batter, mixing just until the flour is completely blended. Use a teaspoon to drop dough onto lightly greased cookie sheets, placing the mounds about 2 inches apart. Bake in the preheated oven for 10 to 12 minutes, until lightly browned. The cookies will keep well in a covered cookie container but cool them thoroughly before storing.

MAKES THREE TO FOUR DOZEN.

LEMON SORBET

A delicate, wonderful dessert with the sharp, fruit flavor of sherbet and the smooth creaminess of ice cream, this dessert is also incredibly easy to make. Serve it at teatime in big bowls with a basket of tuiles (see page 170), those curvy French almond cookies, and mint tea. It is also the perfect conclusion to a meal that has had a substantial entrée, such as pork chops and apples in mustard cream sauce and a salad of arugola and julienned white radish.

Since lemons and blueberries have a pleasant affinity, you can occasionally serve the sorbet with fresh blueberry sauce (see below).

WINE SUGGESTION: A fruity Beaujolais.

> 3 cups heavy cream
> 1 cup milk
> 1½ cups sugar
> Juice of 4 large lemons

Beat the cream, milk, and sugar with a hand or electric beater until the sugar dissolves; the mixture will be thin. Place it in the freezer until it begins to solidify. Remove and beat, adding the juice of 4 lemons. Return to the freezer and, when the mixture begins to solidify again, remove and beat a third time. Return to freezer until hardened.

MAKES APPROXIMATELY ONE QUART.

Note: The time it takes for the sorbet to begin to solidify varies considerably, depending on the depth of your container, the type of container used—metal, for instance, will speed up the process—and your freezer. It can take anywhere from 4 to 8 hours.

FRESH BLUEBERRY SAUCE

> 1 pint fresh blueberries
> ¾ cup sugar

Purée blueberries in a blender. Add sugar and blend until it is dissolved. Serve over lemon sorbet.

SERVES FOUR.

LEMON GRANITA

Tiny pellets of icy lemon crystals may be scooped into wine glasses, to be savored slowly with anise-scented crisp *biscotti all' anaci,* Italian anise cookies. Lemon granita is clean and refreshing, and especially welcome after a substantial entrée of roast loin of pork or a traditional choucroute garni, with its hearty meats and sausages and robust cabbage. For an appropriately simple beginning, have a platter of cardboard-thin slices of prosciutto ham and large, fresh, raw white mushrooms, sliced at the last minute and drizzled with a little lemon and plenty of freshly cracked pepper.

WINE SUGGESTION: A chilled, crisp Alsatian Riesling.

> 2 scant cups sugar
> 2 cups water
> 1 cup lemon juice

Combine sugar and water in a saucepan, bring to a boil, then lower heat and simmer for 5 to 6 minutes, until sugar is melted. Cool. Add lemon juice and mix until well blended. Pour into ice-cube trays or a shallow pan, cover with aluminum foil, and place in the freezer. When the mixture starts to freeze at the edges, remove from the freezer and break it up into ice crystals, using a chopper or a metal spoon. Replace the ice crystals in the freezer. Check again in a half-hour or so, and when the mixture has begun to freeze, repeat the chopping process. Do this at least once more to ensure that the mixture forms into tiny pellets of lemon ice. At serving time you may need to chop the mixture gently once more if the granita is frozen too solid. It really depends on your freezer. Spoon the granita into parfait or wine glasses.

SERVES SIX.

STRAWBERRIES A LA CREME FRAMBOISE
(Strawberries in Cream and Raspberry Eau de Vie)

A perfect light dessert after a heavy meal, such as cassoulet prepared with pork sausages, lamb, pea or marrow beans, and stock, seasoned with shallots, garlic, and thyme. Since the cassoulet is a one-dish entrée, all that's needed is a crisp salad of bite-sized pieces of romaine lettuce tossed with sliced raw fennel in a mustard-spiked vinaigrette.

WINE SUGGESTION: A gutsy red French country wine, such as Corbières or Minervois from Languedoc.

> 3 pints fresh, perfect strawberries
> ¼ cup lemon juice
> 1 pint heavy cream
> 2 tablespoons confectioners' sugar
> 4 tablespoons framboise
> Additional confectioners' sugar

Wash strawberries and pat gently with paper towels. Leave stems on for visual appeal or remove them if you prefer. Pile the berries lightly into a deep bowl, sprinkle them with lemon juice, and refrigerate until serving time.

Just before serving, whip the cream until it holds peaks. Add 2 tablespoons confectioners' sugar and the framboise and mix just to blend. Turn the cream into a chilled glass bowl.

Remove strawberries from refrigerator and pile on a round or oval platter. Bring to table with a small bowl of confectioners' sugar and the bowl of framboise-scented whipped cream. Guests help themselves to berries, sugar, and cream.

SERVES EIGHT.

ORANGES AND PINEAPPLE IN LEMON SYRUP

More and more we love fresh fruits for dessert—these are simply prepared to preserve their exquisite flavors. We like to double the recipe and keep the fruit and its luscious syrup in a large glass apothecary jar, which displays the vivid orange and gold of the fruits enticingly. We bring the jar right to the table and spoon out one perfect, whole orange and a segment of pineapple for each portion. We serve the fruit on white porcelain plates, accompanied by a fork and a knife and, for all its simplicity, it makes a delightful and impressive dessert.

6 small navel or Valencia oranges	½ cup lemon juice
1 large, ripe pineapple	3 cups water
2 cups sugar	¼ cup apple brandy

Peel oranges, making certain to remove all the white, bitter pith, but leave them whole. Trim off the top of the pineapple, cut it lengthwise into halves, then in quarters. Use a sharp knife inserted between the flesh and the skin to pare the pineapple quarters, cutting away any brown flecks or "eyes." Slice each pineapple quarter in half.

Bring the sugar, lemon juice, and water to a boil in a heavy 3-quart saucepan. Lower the heat and simmer the syrup for 15 minutes. Add the whole oranges and pineapple segments and simmer for 10 more minutes, turning the fruits once or twice so that they poach evenly.

Using a slotted spoon, lift out the fruits and place them in a glass jar with a lid. Continue to cook the syrup over brisk heat another 10 to 15 minutes, until it becomes lightly syrupy. Then take off heat and cool. Strain through a fine sieve into the jar with the fruits. Add the brandy. The jar may be stored at room temperature in cool weather, or in an air-conditioned room, or kept in the refrigerator. When serving, spoon 1 whole orange and a segment of pineapple into individual dishes and add a little of the syrup.

SERVES SIX.

BANANES AUX CONFITURES
(Bananas in Cream and Lemon Jelly)

Layers of bananas, lemon jelly, blanched almonds, and whipped cream are the elements of this unusual dessert. Assemble it in an attractive bowl and refrigerate it until the end of the meal when it is brought to the table, tossed gently, and served.

It might follow an entrée of calves' brains and black butter accompanied by braised cucumbers and a watercress and beet salad.

WINE SUGGESTION: A light red wine, such as an Italian Valpolicella or a Bordeaux Supérieur from the Médoc.

> 3 large bananas, peeled and cut into ½-inch slices
> ½ pint lemon jelly (recipe follows)
> 3 tablespoons blanched, slivered almonds
> ½ pint heavy cream, whipped

Place banana slices in the bottom of an attractive serving bowl and cover with lemon jelly. Sprinkle slivered almonds over the jelly and cover with the whipped cream. Refrigerate for 1 hour. Mix carefully, as you would a salad, just before serving.

SERVES FOUR.

LEMON JELLY

There is no pectin in this delectably tart jelly; the natural properties of the fruits do the jelling. It is a pretty apricot color when done and would be delicious served with tiny hot pecan buns or roasted sesame bread and strong, black coffee.

> 6 lemons, peeled and sliced
> 2 cups apples, peeled, cored, and diced
> ¾ cup sugar for each cup of juice

Place lemon slices and apples in the bottom of a saucepan. Press down with a large spoon so that the juices are released. If the juices do not cover the fruit, add a little water. Bring the mixture slowly to a boil and cook until fruit is soft. Put into a damp jelly bag—cheesecloth shaped into a bag—and let the fruit drip into a bowl. Measure ¾ cup sugar for each cup of juice that has dripped into the bowl. Discard pulp. Place juice and sugar in a saucepan. Stir until dissolved and then cook, uncovered, over medium-low heat until the jelly sheets from a spoon. The jelly will still be somewhat runny when it sheets from or coats the spoon, but it jells very quickly as it cools.

MAKES ABOUT 1½ CUPS.

LEMON CREPES FLAMED WITH COGNAC

The lemon juice used as part of the liquid in these crêpes makes them tart and meltingly tender. The delicate crêpes are folded into little triangles, flecked with sugared, grated lemon zest, then bathed in flaming Cognac. The crêpes may be made ahead and rewarmed in the oven before serving. They make a light and lovely little dessert. For a quickly-put-together dinner, serve individual shell steaks garnished with grilled mushroom caps, sprigs of dewy fresh watercress, and baked tomato halves dusted with freshly ground pepper and a little oregano.

WINE SUGGESTION: A Côtes du Rhone or California Petite Sirah with the shell steaks.

THE CRÊPES

2 whole eggs
1 egg yolk
½ cup lemon juice
½ cup cold water

1 cup flour, sifted twice
1 tablespoon sugar
2 tablespoons butter, melted

Beat the 2 eggs and the egg yolk until light and lemon colored, using a whisk or electric beater. Add the lemon juice and cold water and beat until light. Add the sifted flour and the sugar, beating until perfectly smooth and free of lumps. Add the melted butter and mix until smooth. The batter may be placed in the refrigerator for a half hour to help it "set," or you can mix it up in the morning and cook the crêpes later in the day. You can also cook the crêpes ahead of time, stack them with aluminum foil between each crêpe, and keep them in the refrigerator until ready to use. Then warm the previously made crêpes in the oven for 10 minutes.

Use about 2 tablespoons of the batter for each 6-inch crêpe and cook them according to the crêpe pan you have. We like a Teflon pan, which requires no additional oil or butter. Otherwise you will need to add a bit of butter from time to time to prevent the crêpes from sticking to the pan.

THE TOPPING

Grated zest of 2 lemons
3 tablespoons sugar
Have ready ¾ cup Cognac

Fold the cooked crêpes in half, then into quarters, and place in a large skillet or chafing dish. Sprinkle the grated lemon zest and sugar mixture over the tops and heat gently over low flame for a few minutes. Warm the Cognac in a small saucepan. Pour over the crêpes, shaking the pan to distribute the Cognac. Set aflame and serve.

MAKES ABOUT EIGHTEEN CRÊPES, OR ENOUGH TO SERVE FOUR TO SIX.

ZABAGLIONE

One of the delights of this dessert is its frothiness and the speed with which it can be made. Marsala wine, lemon juice, sugar, and egg yolks are whisked to slightly thickened fluffiness, then served either warm or cold, in individual glasses.

It can be made ahead but is nice to keep in mind for those times when you need an impromptu dessert. If this is to be the conclusion to an unexpected meal, your entrée could be pasta, tossed in a cream sauce and then tossed again with diced raw zucchini and slivers of prosciutto ham, accompanied by a salad of romaine lettuce in vinaigrette.

WINE SUGGESTION: A vigorous, dry red Chianti.

6 egg yolks
½ cup sugar
½ cup Marsala wine
Lemon juice

You will need a double boiler, or its equivalent, for the zabaglione. Beat the egg yolks and sugar in the top of the double boiler, off the heat, until thick and pale.

Pour Marsala wine into a measuring cup to the ½-cup mark. Then add enough lemon juice to reach the ⅔ mark. Beat the liquid into the egg-yolk mixture and place over hot water. Continue to beat—a whisk is best for this because it reaches all areas of the pan—until the mixture foams and thickens. Pour into glasses if you are going to serve immediately. If you plan to serve it cold, continue to beat off the heat until it cools slightly. This will make it more creamy and smooth when chilled.

SERVES FOUR.

BLACK-WALNUT LEMON BREAD

Black walnuts give this quick bread a richer, deeper walnut flavor, but you may substitute regular California walnuts with excellent results. The loaf is rich and moist but not overly sweet, nor is the lemon aggressive, here adding an elusive, fresh flavor. It's a perfect bread for a light salad luncheon, to enjoy with afternoon tea, or have toasted with breakfast coffee. Most quick breads dry out easily, but we find this one will keep nicely for four or five days if tightly wrapped or placed in an airtight container. We like the nuts finely ground because this gives an even, pleasing texture.

¼ pound sweet butter (1 stick), softened
1 cup sugar
2 large eggs
2 scant cups flour, sifted before measuring
2 rounded teaspoons baking powder

½ teaspoon baking soda
¼ teaspoon salt
⅓ cup lemon juice
½ cup buttermilk
1 cup black walnuts, finely chopped

Preheat oven to 350° F.

Have all ingredients at room temperature. Cream the softened butter with the sugar until well blended, then add the eggs, one at a time, beating well until blended and light. Sift together the sifted, measured flour, baking powder, baking soda, and salt. Add the sifted flour mixture to the batter alternately with the lemon juice and the buttermilk, beating just enough to blend. Start and end with the flour. Lastly, gently fold in the nuts, just until blended. Don't overbeat or the texture of the bread will be affected. Turn the batter into a greased 5-by-9-inch loaf pan and bake in the preheated oven for 50 minutes to 1 hour, or until the top is golden brown and the sides pull away from the pan. Cool on a rack and store covered.

MAKES EIGHTEEN ½-INCH SLICES.

Note: Don't be alarmed if the mixture should curdle a little when the lemon juice is added. If this happens, immediately fold in a little flour. The dough will rehomogenize, or come together, again.

SAUCES,
STOCKS,
AND PRESERVES

BUTTERSCOTCH LEMON SAUCE

There is nothing like a suave, creamy butterscotch sauce to turn a simple fruit or ice cream into an epicurean treat.

This particular butterscotch sauce is easy to make and always turns out the same way—buttery and delicious. It's perfect over poached pears or apple slices and, along with a handful of toasted hazelnuts, turns vanilla ice cream into an old-fashioned sundae. It is also delicious over ripe, whole strawberries.

This kind of dessert can follow almost anything, but it would be very good after a lovely cheese soufflé accompanied by a Caesar salad.

WINE SUGGESTION: A New York State Seyval Blanc.

> 5 tablespoons butter
> 1 cup brown sugar
> ⅓ cup heavy cream
> 1 tablespoon plus 1 teaspoon lemon juice

Melt butter in a saucepan and add the sugar. Stir briefly and add the cream. Continue cooking over medium heat, stirring occasionally, until mixture comes to a boil and is thick. Stir in the lemon juice.

MAKES ABOUT 1½ CUPS OF BUTTERSCOTCH SAUCE.

LEMON CAPER SAUCE

We like this sauce spooned into the hollow of steamed artichokes, but it is also a super dressing for fresh asparagus, cauliflower, or cold, boiled shrimp.

¾ cup light olive oil
⅓ cup lemon juice
2 tablespoons capers, drained
   and finely chopped
1 hard boiled egg, finely
   grated

1 teaspoon fresh tarragon,
   finely minced, or
   ¼ teaspoon dried
3 cornichons or small
   gherkins, drained and
   finely minced
Salt and freshly ground
   pepper

Combine the oil and lemon juice in a small bowl and beat with a wire whisk until blended. Continue to beat with the whisk as you add the remaining ingredients. Pour into a jar and chill until ready to use. The dressing may be made in a blender, but it will lose the bitey texture that gives it distinction.

MAKES APPROXIMATELY ONE CUP.

HOLLANDAISE SAUCE

If we had to select one sauce for its deliciousness and adaptability to almost any kind of dish, it would be a hollandaise.

Contrary to the widespread belief that it is tricky to make, hollandaise is actually quite easy to prepare and can be done fairly quickly. This lemon-accented, butter-rich sauce is wonderful with a perfectly poached salmon, with either poached or broiled bass, with vegetables—broccoli, asparagus, or cauliflower —with sliced, cold ham, and with egg dishes, such as eggs Benedict.

4 egg yolks
2½ tablespoons lemon juice
¼ pound of butter, cut into 4 pieces
½ teaspoon salt

In the top of a double boiler, off the heat, beat the 4 egg yolks briefly. Add lemon juice, mix well, and place over barely simmering, not boiling, water. Add 1 piece of butter and stir until it has almost melted. Then add a second piece of butter, again stirring constantly until melted. Repeat the procedure with the remaining pieces of butter. Continue stirring until the hollandaise coats the spoon or whisk. Remove from heat, add salt, and continue stirring until the sauce has cooled slightly.

Should the hollandaise start to curdle, lift the top of the double boiler out and take 1 tablespoon of the boiling water from the lower container, and add it to the hollandaise. Return the sauce to the heat, whisk briskly, and it will return to its emulsified state.

The hollandaise can be reheated safely after refrigeration if placed in the top of a double boiler over warm water and whisked. If the sauce separates, add a few drops of boiling water and whisk vigorously.

MAKES ONE HALF-PINT.

LEMON VINAIGRETTE

This basically simple salad dressing is, we think, the very best. A traditional vinaigrette uses vinegar, but unless you have a truly superb vinegar, a lemon vinaigrette has a much better chance of always being good.

We differ on the proportions of oil to lemon juice, so we are giving you both versions, as well as the best way to make mustard vinaigrette.

Once you ascertain what proportion of lemon to oil you prefer, it becomes very easy to make this dressing; your eye will tell you when it is right. Then it becomes a matter or taste if you want to add herbs, garlic, or spices.

½ cup lemon juice		¼ cup lemon juice
1 cup olive oil	Or	1 cup olive oil
½ teaspoon salt		½ teaspoon salt
Freshly ground pepper to taste		Freshly ground pepper to taste

Combine all ingredients and beat well with a small wire whisk or spoon.

MAKES ENOUGH TO DRESS A SALAD FOR TWELVE.

To make a mustard vinaigrette, put the lemon juice in a bowl and add 1 tablespoon of Dijon or Pommery mustard. Beat with a spoon; the mustard will melt into the lemon juice so that when you add the olive oil, everything will amalgamate. If you add the mustard after the oil and lemon juice have been mixed, the mustard will be suspended in small globules no matter how hard you whisk.

If you mix your vinaigrette in this quantity, it's best to add any herbs or other flavorings just before you dress your salad. Any one of the following will zip up your dressing.

1 clove garlic, finely minced
3 medium-sized mushrooms, sliced paper-thin
1 teaspoon dried chervil
2 tablespoons Italian parsley, finely minced
3 artichoke hearts, minced

1 celery heart, cut into julienne strips
½ small, raw zucchini, finely diced
2 scallions or 2 shallots, finely minced

Here are some salad ideas:

SALAD I

2 small, crisp green apples
8 scallions, chopped
4 large Belgian endives, chopped
½ cup mustard vinaigrette

Core apples, but do not peel. Cut them into slices and toss with chopped scallions, endives, and mustard vinaigrette.

SERVES FOUR.

SALAD II

½ pound fresh bean sprouts
4 large Belgian endives, coarsely chopped
1 cup red radishes, sliced
4 scallions, chopped
½ cup mustard vinaigrette

Toss all ingredients with the mustard vinaigrette and serve. If your ingredients are going to sit together in a salad bowl before being tossed, leave the radishes out until the last minute—unless you want a pink salad. Also, with this or any salad, the ingredients must be dry in order to take on the salad dressing properly.

SERVES FOUR.

LEMON MAYONNAISE

It's convenient—and very satisfying—to be able to make your own mayonnaise quickly and easily. It tastes so much better than commercial varieties, it's worth the few minutes it takes to make it.

We use an electric hand-mixer to make this mayonnaise, but you can use a blender or even a spoon. The essential thing is to add the oil very slowly to the egg yolks at the beginning so the mixture will coalesce.

This mayonnaise is lovely served in a bowl surrounded by

fresh, raw vegetables, such as cauliflower flowerets, strips of green pepper, scallions, and carrots. Or try it over fresh, young garden beets that have been steamed in a little water until just tender and then brought to room temperature.

2 egg yolks
¼ teaspoon salt
1 to 2 tablespoons lemon juice
1 to 1½ cups olive oil or vegetable oil (see Note)

Put egg yolks into a bowl that has been rinsed out with hot water and dried thoroughly, and beat them until very pale. Add salt and lemon juice and beat until well incorporated. Starting with a drop at a time, add the oil, beating well after each addition. When the mixture is the consistency of heavy cream, you can add the oil in larger splashes.

How much oil you use will depend partially on how stiff you want the mayonnaise to be. It will take at least 1 cup. If by some chance the mixture curdles, add 1 tablespoon boiling water and beat furiously. The mixture will come together again.

If you wish, you can add minced, fresh herbs to the mayonnaise once it is done.

MAKES ABOUT 1½ CUPS.

Note: There is mild controversy about what kind of oil to use for mayonnaise. Some are adamant that a really good olive oil is necessary. Others feel that if you are using a strong flavoring element, such as lemon or a wonderful vinegar, it shouldn't have to vie with the taste of the olive oil; therefore, a bland vegetable oil is better. Actually, we use both, depending on the dish the mayonnaise will complement.

BEEF STOCK

This makes a rich, beef-flavored stock for soups, sauces, and gravies. No salt is used in any basic stock to permit seasoning to taste in the final recipes.

4 pounds beef bones

3 medium-sized onions, peeled but left whole

2 pounds chuck or brisket

3 medium-sized carrots, scraped and cut into chunks

1 large parsnip, scraped and cut into chunks

1 bouquet garni: Tie together in a square or cheesecloth with a piece of white thread 6 sprigs of parsley, 3 stalks of celery, half a bay leaf, and ⅛ teaspoon thyme

5 quarts water

To give the stock rich color and flavor, the bones and the onions must be browned first. Place the bones in a shallow roasting pan and roast at high heat, 500° F., for 20 to 30 minutes, turning them so they color evenly. When well browned, transfer bones to a 2-gallon stockpot. While the bones are browning, place the peeled onions in a heavy pan, preferably one with a Teflon lining, and cook them over high heat until densely colored; in fact, if they burn a bit, this is all to the good. Add these to the stockpot along with the piece of brisket, the vegetables, the bouquet garni, and the water. Bring to a boil, lower heat to barely simmering, and place the cover on the pot so that it covers about three-quarters of the surface. Simmer quietly for 4 to 4½ hours, skimming scum that arises from time to time. If the stock still seems thin at the end of 4½ hours, continue to simmer another hour or so. Remove the bouquet garni and cool the stock. Take out and discard the bones. There is no point to keeping the meat, since all of its flavor and nutritional values have gone into the stock. Strain the stock through a fine mesh sieve. Pour into containers and refrigerate several hours or overnight; then carefully remove all the congealed fat from the surface. The stock is now ready to use. It will keep 2 weeks in the refrigerator or 6 to 8 months in the freezer.

MAKES ABOUT THREE QUARTS.

GLACE DE VIANDE

This is a concentrated meat jelly prepared by reducing beef stock to a jelly-like consistency. A teaspoon or so of glace de viande enriches soups and sauces. It freezes well into a consistency that can be spooned very easily from the jar. It's handy to keep a small jar of glace de viande in the freezer.

Place 2 quarts home-prepared beef stock (see page 194) in a saucepan. Cook, uncovered, over medium heat until the liquid has reduced to a syrup that sheets from the spoon. This will take several hours. Keep an eye on the mixture during the last stages of cooking, and stir so it won't burn. Cool and store in the refrigerator. It will keep for 2 weeks there, but almost indefinitely in the freezer.

MAKES ONE HALF-PINT.

QUICK, IN-A-PINCH STOCK

If you find yourself out of homemade stock and must use a
canned beef or chicken broth, or dehydrated powders or cubes,
there's a way to get rid of the synthetic taste of these products,
which are heavily endowed with coloring and other additives.

6 sprigs parsley
1 large carrot, scraped and
  cut into thin rounds
1 medium-sized onion, peeled
  and finely chopped

½ cup dry white wine
A pinch of chervil or thyme
Two 14-ounce cans beef or
  chicken broth

Place all ingredients in a heavy 2-quart saucepan, bring to a boil,
lower heat to simmer, and cook with the lid on but not quite covering the entire surface, for 20 minutes. Pour the liquid through
a strainer and cool.

Note: When using this as part of a recipe, reduce the amount
of salt required in the recipe. Canned stock has salt added.

VEAL STOCK

The four basic major stocks—brown or beef, white or veal,
chicken, and fish—lend themselves well to lemon enhancement.
Veal stock, with its gentle yet rich flavor, is well suited to velouté
and other sauces. Like all cooking stocks, the liquid must be
brought to a boil, then kept at a very low heat, barely simmering.

This not only helps retain the natural essences, but it also helps keep the stock clear. Veal bones, especially with bits of meat and gristle clinging to them, evoke a lot of scum. Hence, the first "cleansing," procedure of washing, bringing to a boil, rinsing in cold water, and starting all over again. The barely simmering stock must be skimmed frequently while it cooks.

4 pounds veal knuckle bones, with some meat on them, cut into chunks by the butcher

4 quarts water

2 medium-sized onions, peeled and quartered

2 medium-sized carrots, scraped and cut into slices

1 celery stalk, peeled and sliced

1 bouquet garni: Place in a square of cheesecloth tied with white thread 8 sprigs of parsley, ⅛ teaspoon thyme, 2 peeled cloves garlic, 4 whole cloves, 12 peppercorns, and 1 small bay leaf

Wash the bones in cold water and place them in a large stockpot or Dutch oven. Cover them with cold water. Bring slowly to a boil and boil for 6 minutes. Drain off the water and rinse the bones in cold water again to remove accumulated scum. Wash and dry your stockpot and start again. Place the bones in the pot, add 4 quarts cold water, the vegetables, and the bouquet garni. Bring to a boil, lower heat, cover, and simmer very quietly for 4½ hours, skimming off scum and fat from time to time. Cool and remove the bouquet garni. Strain the stock through a very fine mesh sieve. Pour into a container and refrigerate several hours or overnight; then, using a large spoon, remove the congealed

fat from the surface. The stock is now ready to use. It will keep for 2 weeks in the refrigerator or 6 to 8 months in the freezer.
MAKES ABOUT THREE QUARTS.

BASIC CHICKEN STOCK

Having a good chicken stock on hand is extremely useful. It can be used as the base for a variety of sauces from the classic sauce Parisiènne to any number of pasta sauces. It is also convenient to have for those occasions when you need a moistening agent for roasting, and it is essential to braising.

Unlike most chicken stock recipes, ours has no onion or herbs, which we feel results in a purer stock. Chicken bones are cooked long and slowly in water until the liquid is reduced to the basic essence.

Whenever you have the butcher bone chicken breasts, ask him to give you the bones, for they make an excellent stock.

> Bones and skin from 4 chicken breasts (skin can be omitted)
> or
> 4 chicken wings and 2 chicken necks
> 6 cups water
> ½ cup dry white wine

Place everything but the wine in a kettle and bring to a brisk boil. Skim, reduce heat, and maintain the liquid at a low, though bubbly boil for 45 minutes. Check periodically to see if the stock needs skimming. After 45 minutes add the wine and continue to cook at a low boil, skimming as necessary, for another 30 minutes. Cool, strain and, refrigerate. Skim off congealed fat.

MAKES APPROXIMATELY ONE QUART.

Note: Chicken stock can easily be kept for a week in the refrigerator and, of course, it freezes well. It is helpful to freeze in precise increments, such as ¼-cup quantities. You could put the stock in ice-cube trays, and once frozen, slide them out into plastic bags. Two cubes equal approximately ¼ cup.

PAPRIKA LEMON CREAM SAUCE

The fresh cream and lemon juice in this tangy, creamy, rosy sauce thicken it naturally, without flour. The paprika lends color and a bit of a zip. The sauce is lovely spooned over crisply cooked cauliflower, fresh asparagus spears, or crunchy brussels sprouts.

4 tablespoons butter
2 tablespoons shallots, finely chopped
1¼ cups heavy cream
¼ cup lemon juice

Salt and freshly ground pepper to taste
1 tablespoon sweet red paprika

In a saucepan, melt butter, then add the chopped shallots. Cook over low heat for 3 or 4 minutes, until golden, stirring so the shallots do not burn. Gradually stir in cream and continue to cook over low heat for 5 or 6 minutes. Add lemon juice, salt and pepper, and paprika and continue to cook for another 5 minutes, stirring. When the sauce reaches a medium-thick, creamy consistency, pour over vegetables or serve separately in a sauceboat.

MAKES ONE CUP.

CREME FRAICHE

In France, crème fraîche is a widely used heavy, sweet cream that has been permitted to stand and ripen until it becomes thickened. Its flavor is rich, slightly acidic, and totally unique. In fact, even in France, the cream varies in flavor according to region. Purists here insist that crème fraîche is impossible to reproduce outside of France. It is produced commercially here, but in limited quantities and at inflated prices. However, it is possible to make an American version of crème fraîche at home. It won't taste like the crème fraîche of France, but it is a reasonable reproduction of it and very simple to prepare. We think either of the following recipes results in a serviceable, excellent thickened cream, with good flavor and body. When used to thicken sauces, crème fraîche has the advantage of never curdling; it also makes a delightful cream for fresh berries or puddings.

CREME FRAICHE I

1 pint heavy sweet cream
6 teaspoons buttermilk

Place the heavy cream in a large, sterilized glass jar and stir in the buttermilk until well blended. Cover the jar loosely with its lid. Don't screw it tightly because air must get into the jar. Leave at room temperature—not higher than 85° F. or lower than

60° F.—for 8 hours. Stir the cream to a smooth consistency, cap it tightly, and refrigerate until ready to use.

CREME FRAICHE II

1 pint heavy cream
⅓ cup natural, unpasteurized yogurt

Place the cream in a large, sterilized glass jar. Stir in the yogurt until well blended. Proceed as in Crème Fraîche I.

LEMON CHUTNEY

Sugary little green figs sweeten this chutney and melt into the rich, amber liquid, thick with lemon slices, and blond raisins. This chutney, obviously, is perfect for curries, but it is also lovely served with a loin of pork, roasted with fresh rosemary. Place a bowl of chutney on a tray along with Dijon mustard, a molasses-based mustard, and a plum conserve so your guests can have a choice of sweets and sours with the crusty pork. A salad of cooked, mixed vegetables tossed with a thin mayonnaise dressing makes a nice contrast.

WINE SUGGESTION: A red Graves has a robust earthiness that is great with pork.

1 cup green figs, sliced
2 cups halved lemon slices
1 cup blond raisins
1 cup chopped onions
1 cup sugar
1½ cups cider vinegar

3 tablespoons candied
    ginger, finely chopped
½ teaspoon whole allspice,
    crushed
1 teaspoon salt

Combine all ingredients in a saucepan and bring to a boil. Reduce heat and simmer, covered, for 1 hour. Uncover and simmer for another half-hour, or until thickened.

MAKES ABOUT THREE CUPS.

PINEAPPLE-LEMON PRESERVES

Fresh pineapple, apples, and chopped lemon slices are simmered with sugar until they reach the color of old gold and have melted into one another. This is delicious with hot croissants and strong, rich coffee. The preserves can also be served, warmed slightly, over vanilla ice cream.

2½ cups pineapple, peeled and coarsely chopped
1½ cups Granny Smith apples, peeled, cored, and coarsely chopped
½ cup quartered lemon slices
3 cups sugar
3 tablespoons brandy or Cognac

One good-sized pineapple will provide the amount needed for this recipe. Cut off the spiky top and base and peel off the thorny skin. With a knife cut out any little tough, brown pieces that tend to grow into the fruit. Be sure and chop only the soft part and avoid the hard core.

If Granny Smith apples are not available, any fairly tart apple will do.

Place pineapple and apples into a large pot and cook over low heat for 10 minutes. While the apples and pineapple are cooking, slice, chop, and blanch the lemon. To do this, bring a small pot of water to a high boil, turn off the heat, and add the lemon. After 5 minutes, drain the lemon, being sure to shake off any excess water. Add the blanched lemon and the sugar to the pineapple and apple mixture. Cook over low-to-medium heat for 1½ hours, skimming as necessary. Pour into three half-pint jars and add 1 tablespoon Calvados or other brandy to each jar.

SPICY CRANBERRY SAUCE

Onions, allspice, lemon juice, and vinegar give this cranberry sauce its spicy individuality. The dark garnet color, smooth saucelike texture, and zesty flavor of this condiment make it an especially delectable companion to roast turkey, chicken or pork, cold sliced meats and poultry. It will keep up to a month in the refrigerator in a lidded jar.

½ cup water
½ cup fresh lemon juice
1 cup onions, very finely minced
2 cups sugar
½ cup red wine vinegar

1 tablespoon ground allspice
Salt and freshly ground pepper to taste
2 pounds fresh cranberries

In a large saucepan combine all ingredients except the cranberries. Bring to a boil, lower heat, and simmer for 15 minutes. Add the cranberries and cook until all the berries pop—about 10 minutes. Purée the mixture in a food processor or food mill. Return to the heat and cook over low flame for another 10 to 15 minutes, until thickened. Pour into glass jars and refrigerate until ready to use.

MAKES ABOUT FOUR CUPS.

LEMON BUTTER

Freshly ground white pepper to taste
4 to 5 tablespoons lemon juice
½ pound butter, softened

Add pepper and lemon juice to softened butter and beat with a wooden spoon until well blended and smooth. Turn the mixture into a lidded crock or jar and keep refrigerated.

This will keep about 1 week. To keep longer, shape the lemon butter into a sausage-like roll, wrap securely in freezer wrap or aluminum foil, and place in the freezer. To use, slice off the amount needed, wrap additional foil securely around the open end, and replace immediately in the freezer.

INDEX

Doris Tobias, Food and Wine Editor for Women's Wear Daily *and a regular contributer to* House and Garden *and* American Home, *admits to harboring a secret fantasy in which she plays four-handed piano with Vladimir Horowitz. Meanwhile, she often tests recipes while listening to Saturday broadcasts of The Metropolitan Opera.*

Mary Merris, News Editor for Women's Wear Daily *and a senior editor of* W, *dreams of having a house in the south of France where she will serve good simple food surrounded by flowers and trees, animals and close friends.*